THE DOGS OF DIPLOMACY

Exploring the Radical Geographies of Modern Times

BY DANIELE-HADI IRANDOOST

EDITED, WITH PREFACE, BY DAVID WILLIAM PARRY

THE DOGS OF DIPLOMACY: EXPLORING THE RADICAL GEOGRAPHIES OF MODERN TIMES

Daniele-Hadi Irandoost
Edited, with a Preface, by David William Parry

978-1-7638613-4-3

©Manticore Press, Melbourne, Australia, 2024.

Thema Classification: JP (Politics & Government)

MANTICORE PRESS
WWW.MANTICORE.PRESS

For my partner

DWP

PREVIOUS BOOKS BY DANIELE-HADI IRANDOOST

On the Philosophy of Education: Towards an Anthroposophical View

A New Vision of Spycraft: Or Necessary Notations on Espionage

Rahab's House of Spies: Covert Action, Military Intelligence, and Espionage Oversight

CONTENTS

∼

LIST OF FIGURES

Archiwum Cyfrowe [National Digital Archives]. Artwork in the public domain; image retrieved from Szukaj w Archiwach [Search the Archives]. https://www.szukajwarchiwach.gov.pl/en/jednostka/-/jednostka/5973991/obiekty/448467#opis_obiektu.

2.1. *Pat Nixon Stands with Premier Chou En-Lai in the Great Hall of the People's Banquet Hall*. February 21, 1972. Photograph. NAID no. 40508862, Nixon White House Photographs, January 20, 1969–August 9, 1974, White House Photo Office Collection (Nixon Administration), January 20, 1969–August 9, 1974, Richard Nixon Library, Yorba Linda, CA. Artwork in the public domain; image retrieved from the National Archives Catalog. https://catalog.archives.gov/id/40508862.

2.2. *Mao, Bulganin, Stalin, Ulbricht Tsedenbal*. December 21, 1949. Photograph, 1,663 × 1,092 pixels. Wikimedia Commons. Artwork in the public domain; image retrieved from Wikimedia Commons. https://commons.wikimedia.org/wiki/File:Mao,_Bulganin,_Stalin,_Ulbricht_Tsedenbal.jpeg#.

2.3. *John Leighton Stuart1948*. 1948. Photograph, 867 × 1,062 pixels. Wikimedia Commons. Artwork in the public domain; image retrieved from Wikimedia Commons. https://commons.wikimedia.org/wiki/File:John_Leighton_Stuart1948.jpg.

3.1. Bain News Service. *Zeppelin Passenger Ship*. ca. 1910–1915. Photograph, glass negative, 5 × 7 in. or smaller. Reproduction no. LC-DIG-ggbain-09494, George Grantham Bain Collection, Prints and Photographs Division, Library of Congress, Washington, DC. Artwork in the public domain; image retrieved from the Library of Congress. https://www.loc.gov/item/2014689480/.

3.2. Wmpearl [pseud.]. *'The Fall of Icarus', 17th Century, Musée Antoine Vivenel*. 2010. Sculpture. Musée Antoine Vivenel. Artwork in the public domain; image retrieved from Wikimedia Commons. https://commons.wikimedia.org/wiki/File:%27The_Fall_of_Icarus%27,_17th_century,_Mus%C3%A9e_Antoine_Vivenel.JPG#.

3.3. Pennell, Joseph. *That Liberty Shall Not Perish from the Earth - Buy Liberty Bonds Fourth Liberty Loan / / Joseph Pennell del. ; Ketterlinus Phila. imp.* 1918. Poster, black and white film copy negative, 104 × 75 cm. Reproduction no. LC-USZ62-57932, World War I Posters, Prints and Photographs Division, Library of Congress, Washington, DC. Artwork in the public domain; image retrieved from the Library of Congress. https://www.loc.gov/item/2002712077/.

4.1. Groov3 [pseud.]. *Palais des Nations unies, à Genève* [United Nations Palace, Geneva]. June 25, 2017. Photograph, 2,672 × 2,138 pixels. Wikimedia Commons. Artwork in the public domain; image retrieved from Wikimedia

Commons. https://commons.wikimedia.org/wiki/File:Palais_des_Nations_unies,_%C3%A0_Gen%C3%A8ve.jpg.

4.2. de Broen, Willem. *Portret van Hugo de Groot* [Portrait of Hugo Grotius]. ca. 1705–1748. Etching and engraving, 187 × 115 mm. Object no. RP-P-1905-1569, Rijksmuseum, Amsterdam. Artwork in the public domain; image retrieved from the Rijksmuseum. https://id.rijksmuseum.nl/200166298.

4.3. Bosse, Abraham. *Leviathan, or the Matter, Forme, & Power of a Common-wealth, Ecclesiasticall and Civill.* 1651. Line engraving. ID no. 055054, British Library, London. Artwork in the public domain; image retrieved from British Library's Flickr Collection. https://www.flickr.com/photos/britishlibrary/12458803675/in/photostream/.

5.1. Profpcde [pseud.]. *European Parliament Hemicycle - Brussels 2024.* November 11, 2024. Photograph, 4,032 × 3,024 pixels. Wikimedia Commons. Artwork in the public domain; image retrieved from Wikimedia Commons. https://commons.wikimedia.org/wiki/File:European_Parliament_Hemicycle_-_Brussels_2024.jpg.

5.2. Romaine [pseud.]. *Brussels-Berlaymont Building (1).* 2018. Photograph, 4,032 × 2,268 pixels. Wikimedia Commons. Artwork in the public domain; image retrieved from Wikimedia Commons. https://commons.wikimedia.org/wiki/File:Brussels-Berlaymont_building_(1).jpg.

6.1. *President Ronald Reagan and Soviet General Secretary Gorbachev Signing the INF Treaty in the East Room.* December 8, 1987. Photograph. NAID no. 75855867, Reagan White House Photographs, January 20, 1981–January 20, 1989, White House Photographic Collection, January 20, 1981–January 20, 1989, Ronald Reagan Library, Simi Valley, CA. Artwork in the public domain; image retrieved from the National Archives Catalog. https://catalog.archives.gov/id/75855867.

6.2. Rowe, Abbie. *Truman Signing North Atlantic Treaty Proclamation.* August 24, 1949. Photograph. NAID no. 338957530, Photographs Relating to the Administration, Family, and Personal Life of Harry S. Truman, 1957–2023, Photograph Collection, 1957–2023, Harry S. Truman Library, Independence, MO. Artwork in the public domain; image retrieved from the National Archives Catalog. https://catalog.archives.gov/id/338957530.

7.1. *ChristianAndMuslimPlayingChess.* ca. 1251–1283. Painting. In *Les croisades: origines et conséquences*, by Claude Lebédel, 108. Rennes: Ouest-France, 2006. Artwork in the public domain; image retrieved from Wikimedia Commons. https://commons.wikimedia.org/wiki/File:ChristianAndMuslimPlayingChess.JPG#.

7.2. en:User:Aivazovsky [pseud.]. *Location Nagorno-Karabakh.* May 1, 2006. Map. Wikimedia Commons. Map in the public domain; image retrieved from Wikimedia Commons. https://en.wikipedia.org/wiki/File:Location_Nagorno-Karabakh.png.

7.3. Zadig, Bertrand. *Oswald Spengler Woodcut.* 1926. Wood cut. *Washington Post*, May 16, 1926. Artwork in the public domain; image retrieved from Wikimedia Commons. https://commons.wikimedia.org/wiki/File:Oswald_Spengler_woodcut.jpg.

8.1. Thomas, Lowell [or Harry Chase]. *With Lawrence in Arabia (1924) Frontispiece.* 1918. Photograph, 2,050 × 2,932 pixels. In *With Lawrence in Arabia*, by Lowell Thomas, frontispiece. New York: Century, 1924. Artwork in the public domain; image retrieved from Wikimedia Commons. https://commons.wikimedia.org/wiki/File:With_Lawrence_in_Arabia_(1924)_frontispiece.png.

8.2. Pingstone, Adrian. *Portmeirion.750pix.* June 2, 2003. Photograph, 750 × 563 pixels. Wikimedia Commons. Artwork in the public domain; image retrieved from Wikimedia Commons. https://commons.wikimedia.org/wiki/File:Portmeirion.750pix.jpg.

10.1. Hine, Lewis Wickes. *Photograph of a Workman on the Framework of the Empire State Building.* 1930. Photograph, 3,000 × 2,401 pixels. NAID no. 518290, General Print File of the National Research Project, 1936–1940, Records of the Work Projects Administration, 1922–1944, National Archives at College Park, College Park, MD. Artwork in the public domain; image retrieved from Wikimedia Commons. https://commons.wikimedia.org/wiki/File:Old_timer_structural_worker2.jpg.

10.2. Wilfredor [pseud.]. *Hong Kong at Night B&W.* August 6, 2013. Photograph, 3,854 × 1,729 pixels. Wikimedia Commons. Artwork in the public domain; image retrieved from Wikimedia Commons. https://commons.wikimedia.org/wiki/File:Hong_Kong_at_night_B%26W.jpg.

10.3. Bach, Eviatar. *Occupy Vancouver Signs.* October 20, 2011. Photograph, 3,648 × 2,736 pixels. Wikimedia Commons. Artwork in the public domain; image retrieved from Wikimedia Commons. https://commons.wikimedia.org/wiki/File:Occupy_Vancouver_signs.jpg.

11.1. Bentham, Jeremy. *Panopticon.* 1791. Plan, 2,179 × 2,402 pixels. Wikimedia Commons. Artwork in the public domain; image retrieved from Wikimedia Commons. https://commons.wikimedia.org/wiki/File:Panopticon.jpg.

13.1. Knight, Arthur. *Philip K Dick in Early 1960s (Photo by Arthur Knight) (Cropped)*. 1962 [or earlier]. Photograph, 3,074 × 4,000 pixels. Wikimedia Commons. Artwork in the public domain; image retrieved from Wikimedia Commons. https://commons.wikimedia.org/wiki/File:Philip_K_Dick_in_ early_1960s_(photo_by_Arthur_Knight)_(cropped).jpg.

13.2. *Gramsci foto segnaletica* [Gramsci Photo Signaling]. 1933. Photograph, 1,331 × 826 pixels. Wikimedia Commons. Artwork in the public domain; image retrieved from Wikimedia Commons. https://commons.wikimedia.org/ wiki/File:Gramsci_foto_segnaletica.jpg.

14.1. *Air France Flight 4721 - Ruhollah Khomeini's Return to Iran*. February 1, 1979. Photograph, 999 × 646 pixels. Institute for Iranian Contemporary Historical Studies, Tehran. Artwork in the public domain; image retrieved from Wikimedia Commons. https://commons.wikimedia.org/wiki/File:Air_ France_Flight_4721_-_Ruhollah_Khomeini%27s_return_to_Iran.jpg.

14.2. Jean-Léon Gérôme. *Prayer in the Mosque*. 1871. Oil on canvas, 35 × 29 1/2 in. (88.9 × 74.9 cm). Object no. 87.15.130., Catharine Lorillard Wolfe Collection, Bequest of Catharine Lorillard Wolfe, 1887, European Paintings, Metropolitan Museum of Art, New York. Artwork in the public domain; image retrieved from the Met. https://www.metmuseum.org/art/collection/ search/436482.

15.1. Kennerly, David Hume. *Gerald and Betty Ford Meet with Deng Xiaoping, 1975 A7598-20A*. December 3, 1975. Photograph, 6,000 × 3,844 pixels. Gerald R. Ford Presidential Library and Museum. Artwork in the public domain; image retrieved from Wikimedia Commons. https://commons.wikimedia.org/ wiki/File:Gerald_and_Betty_Ford_meet_with_Deng_Xiaoping,_1975_A7598- 20A.jpg#.

A PREFACE OF ARTEFACTS AGAINST HISTORY

BY DAVID WILLIAM PARRY

Artefacts are everything. An insight I discerned from early readings of Martin Heidegger as a somewhat insecure teenager. And, as such, one could say artefacts are the veritable shadows of *Sein und Zeit*, while also working as political vortices framing our psychocultural expectations by their very presence in everyday affairs.

Espied so, artefacts are akin to guardian angels, or protective memorabilia, against our continually decaying sense of history. Hence, they ironically help to form the unlimited semiosis of fantasy, the veritable marrow of conceptual truth, and each enshrined fact characterizing the chaos otherwise known as international relations. Indeed, if grasped correctly, artifaction is discovered in those hidden but expressive, processes inhering courtly manners, ambassadorial French, anthropological theater, maps, fictional discourses and unequal futurologies.

All meaning, *The Dogs of Diplomacy: Exploring the Radical Geographies of Modern Times* as a new book by the rapidly rising young author, Daniele-Hadi Irandoost, is a multileveled volume exploring unexpected historiographical evidence and economic folktales from a number of competing narratives. In these senses, Irandoost's text, *The Dogs of Diplomacy: Exploring the Radical Geographies of Modern Times*, clearly identifies the ideological hallmarks of powerful elites who tend to see the world around them as merely standing-reserve, instead of a religious meeting ground that slowly manifests our infinite human potential.

So, almost without rest, Irandoost examines paradoxical social identities via his studies of documents, global politics, regional economic inequality and literary fiction in order to reveal macrocosmic signs within the *unus mundus* itself. So grasped, his readers can sympathize with everyone who perceives suggestive analogies or encoded writ in Irandoost's delvings into such inscribed microcosmic substructures. Ultimately, my allied sympathies confessed, due to a shared inkling these abiding *objets d'art* are transfigurative installations already inside metaphysical dimensions located elsewhere, not to mention literal embodiments of motive and intent on these pragmatic, existential planes.

In which case, I do not have the slightest hesitation in recommending this delightful and truly absorbing book, *The Dogs of Diplomacy: Exploring the Radical Geographies of Modern Times*, to anyone who wants to learn more about our current age, or artifacts—while simultaneously investigating the often-grim pneumatics through which our world actually operates.

Rev. David William Parry
Bute 2025

PART I

GLOBAL HISTORY AND FANTASY MAPS

CHAPTER I

THE FAILURE OF THE UNITED STATES AND BRITAIN TO DETER JAPAN FROM GOING TO WAR IN 1941

1941, December 7/8. The Imperial Japanese Navy Air Service attacked Pearl Harbor and invaded the mainland of British Malaya. The Pacific War was then begun, and the war was continued by the entry of the United States on the side of the Allies.[1] In this chapter, I shall account for the causes which helped to give way to war in this new theatre, in spite of the old opposition and deterrence measures, including the intervention of diplomacy to sanction, by the United States and the British Empire and Commonwealth, by which course Japan lost trade connections with the Western powers, as well as with the Middle East and South America; and the consequence was that Imperial Japan was deprived of the resources it required to maintain its industrial production.[2] Besides, being subjected to heavier encirclement, the Allied coalition accordingly helped the Republic of China against this empire, notwithstanding that Japan had attained supremacy over the mainland territories of China by force.

Only a brief account can be here given of all the deterrence operations delivered to Japan by the United States, the British Empire, and other powers; but to answer the question concerning the origins of the war in eastern Asia, the Pacific Ocean, the Indian Ocean, and Oceania, we must trace from what conditions and mechanisms the leaders of the Empire of Japan derived their decided mission. In this respect, we must certainly review the external and internal circumstances impressed on the inhabitants of Japan. Therefore, when we enter upon the history and records of that period, we find the excited imagination acting upon the proudest leaders of the rising empire—to become the light of Asia, the protector of Asia, and the leader of Asia.

Figure 1.1. Photograph taken from a Japanese plane during the torpedo attack on ships moored on both sides of Ford Island.

Historical Legacies

Before examining the mechanisms attending the start of the Asia-Pacific War, it is necessary to confess that the origins of the war may be traced till the second half of the nineteenth century during the breakdown of the "China-centred international system that had dominated East Asia";[3] and immediately, Japan was compelled to reconsider its own place in the region and the political world.[4] In short, the elite of the nation became disposed to transform Japan into a "regional hegemon." Thereafter, the Empire of the Rising Sun did not miss its opportunity to oppose the incursions of the Western ocean outsiders, and to raise itself to influence among the great powers.[5] By the account, indeed, of Best and colleagues, in their *International*

History of the Twentieth Century and Beyond, the officers in the highest branches of the armed forces had a hope of once more freeing their country from the influence of the Western powers, who had struck their economy a severe blow in the dark recesses of the Great Depression in the 1930s.[6] It has been supposed that Japan exchanged the ideas of the white nations for "a new order at home and expansion overseas in order to overcome the problems of modernization."[7] Japan then proceeded with the advance of "military adventures in East Asia and, in addition, its export of cheap consumer goods to the European colonial empires," which, accurately enquired into, "directly challenged Western interests and provoked substantial hostility" toward the Japanese.[8] It appeared, then, perceiving that there remained no more but to build an empire capable of resisting the colonial hands of white, presumptuous men, they resolved to charge their military to reinforce the authority of Japan over the region.

Accordingly, in process of time, Japan was changed into a military dictatorship, which, indeed, afforded pretext to decide to enter the war.[9] We are further informed that the plight of the peasantry favored the progress of transforming the democratic form of government.[10] Yet, in practice— considering the times in which they lived—the source of this species of militarism was in the oppression of the economic slump, dictated by the Great Depression.[11] Apparently, with this observation, the top officers in the armed services concluded that "national renewal and economic prosperity were to be found in the rediscovery of Japanese pride at home and in the reassertion of Japanese power abroad";[12] and this rendered it impossible to comply with the opinions and demands of the foreign nations—a circumstance which plainly shows that the conditional causes of the Asia-Pacific War originated in the domestic affairs of this country.

Britain and Japan

In this section, I shall take a view of the political connexion between Japan and the British Empire before the war broke out. Upon the whole, the Anglo-Japanese relations became gradually corrupted from "acrimony to confrontation and finally to conflict."[13] But more particularly to illustrate this conjecture, one could tell of the narrative of "the differences over trade, the naval rivalry and the controversy over Japan's links with the Axis."[14] However, from another interpretation, we are given to understand that one of the principal points of contention related to "power and in particular power over the commercial destiny of China."[15] In the meantime, tensions grew especially after Japan rejected the Nine-Power Treaty and announced their preconcerted purpose of establishing the "New Order in East Asia."[16]

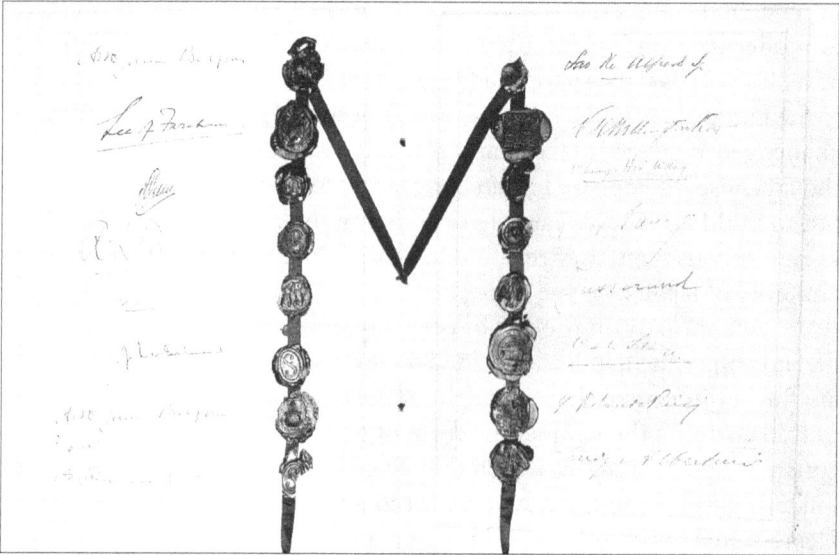

Figure 1.2. Nine-Power Treaty, signed on October 14, 1937.

In consequence of these proceedings, which then undermined its power and position, Britain, at the end of 1938, began to assist China in its defense against Japan. But what is worse, the Molotov-Ribbentrop Pact greatly provoked the spite of the old parliamentary leaders, who, in their turn, resolved to increase their economic warfare against nations not yet formally engaged in the conflict, such as Japan.[17] In this manner, the hostility between the two countries became more widely displayed when, at the war-trade talks of May and June 1940, Britain asked Japan to "sacrifice its links with Germany," but itself refused to cut off its dealings with Chongqing.[18] It may be remarked also, that tensions further arose in the region, especially since Japan failed to honor the terms of a confidential memorandum signed by Britain, which had obliged it to prohibit the transfer of "arms, ammunition, petrol, trucks, and railway material" to China through the Burma Road, "to secure an equitable peace in the Far East."[19]

Figure 1.3. Soviet Foreign Minister Molotov signs the Nazi-Soviet Pact on August 23, 1939. Behind him stand Joachim von Ribbentrop and Josef Stalin.

Nevertheless, although the regional disputes continued to weaken Anglo-Japanese relations, the Tripartite Pact (September 27, 1940) compelled Britain not to consider Japan as being neutral.[20] Such is the singular story of how Britain, in those unsettled times, pressed upon Japan the inevitable policies of containment—a threat, by the way, which rendered it more difficult to avoid the possibility of a direct war.[21] Moreover, the same sentiment induced the British to persuade other countries to obstruct Japan's acts of expansionism, which the Japanese regarded as the "ABCD encirclement."[22] At last, as was evident, Roosevelt froze Japan's assets and impeded their export of oil.[23] Such being the case, the hostilities broke out four-and-a-half months later.[24]

Narodowe Archiwum Cyfrowe

Figure 1.4. Signing of the Tripartite Pact between Germany, Italy and Japan in Berlin.

Japan and the United States

What perhaps sealed the fate of the nation was the increasing degradation of the diplomatic relations between Japan and the United States. Where, on the one hand, Japan conceived that hegemony over East Asia and Southeast Asia was the only mode in which it could avoid "economic decline and subservience to the European powers that controlled the vital resources of the region,"[25] it is no less evident, on the other, that the Americans became convinced that Japan's control of Chinese and European possessions in

Asia would shift the balance of power in the western Pacific, which was said to inflict calamities upon the "American economic interests in the region."[26] Hence, like the German Empire before the First World War, Japan was tempted to engage in stratagems of preventive war—for, as it conceived, "By the autumn of 1941 the Japanese naval forces in the western Pacific had attained virtual parity in the region with the combined fleets of the United States and Great Britain," though it knew the war-making of these powers appeared greater than its own.[27]

Furthermore, before the Pacific War, some compromise went under way in order to come to a settlement between the United States' embargo on oil and the proposed "withdrawal of Japanese forces from *all* of the territories occupied since 1931 as a *precondition* to a settlement in East Asia" (italics in the original).[28] Nevertheless, although some high officials in Tokyo supported the proposal to collaborate, "no Japanese leader in a position of authority was prepared to relinquish the special position in Manchukuo and China," which had cost so much.[29] Sure enough, they appear to have treated their own defeat in the invasion of China, and surrender to the power of the United States, as a loss of pride and prestige, which would have eroded their privileged position domestically.[30]

Other Arguments

Having thus given some reasons why Japan joined World War II in 1941, we must not omit to state that, in some respects, the world was divided into two blocs: one side consisted of Nazi Germany, the Kingdom of Italy, and Japan; the other comprised the United States, Britain, and China.[31] From this, the tendency to believe in the certainty of a future war was natural, and, the temper of the times considered, seemed connected with the fact that Japan could not change sides.[32] In a word, Japan (or, more properly, the supreme command) "was all set to undertake the Indo-China invasion, and it was too late to reverse that decision."[33] What is more to our present purpose, Japan conceived that it had caught at a "once in a lifetime" opportunity to assert its dominion in East Asia, in light of the defeat of Western colonial powers—namely, Holland and France.[34] The affair, it so happened, rested upon the assumption that the Allied powers were not prepared to wage war in two directions, or fronts.[35]

Overall Evaluation and Conclusion

What is above narrated informs us at length of the general opinions respecting the origins of the Pacific War. We come now briefly to estimate the overall truth of these descriptions.

The general proposition that the sanctions the United States, rather than the Houses of Parliament, influenced the course of events is altogether mistaken, because they were rooted in the indirect policies of the British Empire. It is necessary, in this case, to enter into a discussion of the foreign policies of both the United States and Britain, to which I previously alluded. It is equally absurd to assign the principal blame on the Western powers, when there was already a desire on the part of Japan's leaders to become the strongest empire in the region—as the "liberator" of Asia, and so forth. With this observation, we may conclude that the origins of the Pacific War are to be found in Japan's burst of enthusiasm to be a "regional hegemon," while the shadows of the White House and Parliament were gathering about them.

ENDNOTES

[1]   Antony Best et al., *International History of the Twentieth Century and Beyond*, 2nd ed. (Abingdon, UK: Routledge, 2008), 76.

[2]   Best et al., *International History of the Twentieth Century and Beyond*, 74–75.

[3]   Best et al., *International History of the Twentieth Century and Beyond*, 59.

[4]   Best et al., *International History of the Twentieth Century and Beyond*, 59.

[5]   Best et al., *International History of the Twentieth Century and Beyond*, 59.

[6]   Best et al., *International History of the Twentieth Century and Beyond*, 77.

[7]   Best et al., *International History of the Twentieth Century and Beyond*, 77–78.

[8]   Best et al., *International History of the Twentieth Century and Beyond*, 78.

[9]   William R. Keylor, *The Twentieth-Century World: An International History*, 4th ed. (Oxford: Oxford University Press, 2001), 231.

[10]   Keylor, *The Twentieth-Century World*, 231.

[11]   Keylor, *The Twentieth-Century World*, 231.

[12]   Keylor, *The Twentieth-Century World*, 231.

[13]   Antony Best, *Britain, Japan and Pearl Harbor: Avoiding War in East Asia, 1936–41* (London: Routledge, 1995), 193.

[14]   Best, *Britain, Japan and Pearl Harbor*, 193.

[15]   Best, Britain, *Japan and Pearl Harbor*, 193.

[16]   Best, Britain, *Japan and Pearl Harbor*, 193.

[17]   Best, Britain, *Japan and Pearl Harbor*, 194.

[18]   Best, Britain, *Japan and Pearl Harbor*, 194–5.

[19]   Jie Gao, "Compromise and Defence: Great Britain and the Burma Road Crisis," *China and Asia: A Journal in Historical Studies* 3, no. 1 (2021): 22, https://doi.org/10.1163/2589465X-030102.

[20]   Best, *Britain, Japan and Pearl Harbor*, 195.

[21]   Best, *Britain, Japan and Pearl Harbor*, 195.

[22]   John Stephan, review of *Demystifying Pearl Harbor: A New Perspective from Japan*, by Iguchi Takeo, with a foreword by Akira Iriye, *Journal of Pacific History* 46, no. 1 (2011): 143, https://doi.org/10.1080/00223344.2011.573650.

[23]   Best, *Britain, Japan and Pearl Harbor*, 195–6.

[24]   Best, *Britain, Japan and Pearl Harbor*, 196.

[25]   Keylor, *The Twentieth-Century World*, 241.

[26] Keylor, *The Twentieth-Century World*, 241.

[27] Keylor, *The Twentieth-Century World*, 240.

[28] Keylor, *The Twentieth-Century World*, 240.

[29] Keylor, *The Twentieth-Century World*, 240.

[30] Akira Iriye, *The Origins of the Second World War in Asia and the Pacific* (Harlow, UK: Longman, 1987), 141.

[31] Iriye, *The Origins of the Second World War in Asia and the Pacific*, 141.

[32] Iriye, *The Origins of the Second World War in Asia and the Pacific*, 141.

[33] Iriye, *The Origins of the Second World War in Asia and the Pacific*, 143.

[34] Best et al., *International History of the Twentieth Century and Beyond*, 74.

[35] Best et al., *International History of the Twentieth Century and Beyond*, 74.

CHAPTER II

AMERICAN DIPLOMACY AND THE "LOST CHANCE" THEORY IN MAINLAND CHINA

History is a conspiracy
Of mediocre minds.
—David William Parry, *Caliban's Redemption*

The object of this chapter is to discuss, as historically as I can, the entrenchment of an opinion which some scholars have maintained from the earliest twilight of the People's Republic of China (PRC), after the Chinese Civil War between the Chinese Communist Party (CCP) and the Kuomintang (KMT) had ended in 1949, and which, instead of being an apology for another enforced argument, is urged with growing intensity by its strength of alliance with the Union of Soviet Socialist Republics (USSR) as it previously existed, and the Russian Federation at present—that the chance which regulated the particular diplomatic relation of the United States (US) to China was lost in itself, and is one of the acknowledged points of hindrance to the continued dominance of the West today; and that it should be reinforced by an investigation of new documents, released since the 1950s, to admit the "lost chance" thesis.

The very reasons which have been given to express the theory they have raised show how unavoidable it is. But it does not follow that the inevitability of the case must lie in the hostility of the policies of the United States on which its anti-Communism rested. The difficulty of the case lay in all pro-KMT consensuses, in which there existed real attempts to avoid a war with Korea and Vietnam.[1] And factually, so long as uncustomary opinions are deeply rooted in any myth, they lose rather than gain in advocacy by having an in-depth analysis of the annals of public history. For if it were presented as a result of a conviction, the comparison between the China-US and Sino-Soviet relations might mean it was never viable for the United States to lose China.

What the "Lost Chance" Thesis Is

In every grade of the scale of theory, the conclusion is hard upon those who find an almost universal school. To look at the affirmative side of the thesis: they (the US) had less difficulty in getting a friendly overture, than had any other parties in obtaining significance. If they did put out feelers until 1949, they were subjected to a set of famous conversations totally different from those extracted from others. If there was an example of the possibility of any optimistic open invitation—in which the telegrams of officials in general were prominently featured—as in the case of the ambassador of the United States to China, John Leighton Stuart, and Huang Hua, the director of the Foreign Affairs Office under the Nanjing Municipal Military Control Commission—those who conceive that the interest aroused thereby produced their enthusiasms did so in response to the eagerness of the two diplomats, who had corresponded and were eager to meet; and at no time did they suggest doing aught less than to show that the opportunity afforded by their counterpart was of no value.[2]

Figure 2.1. Pat Nixon stands with Premier Zhou Enlai in the Great Hall of the People's Banquet Hall, on February 21, 1972. Did the United States "lose" China following the Chinese Civil War in 1949?

Again, in other examples, the *onus probandi* was supposed to be with the "Zhou *démarche*," a message sent by Zhou Enlai to the United States, in which he tried to contend for any disposition that might obtain the general aid of that republic.[3] The *à priori* conception was in favor of reconstruction and honesty. It was held that there should be no restraint required by the United States, and that the Soviet Union was no respecter of the Chinese and would not prevent its breakdown.[4] It was not useless for the American Consul General in Beijing, Oliver Edmund Clubb, to say that Zhou, who maintained the optimism that the United States had an attempt to befriend, or that the Soviet Union imposed pressures, was on the affirmative side of the divide.[5]

It was equally pertinent for Clubb to say that those who denied party members any radicalism or liberalism as was theoretically given to Chairman Mao Zedong, and who bore the unanswered argument against them—that the hardliner Liu Shaoqi was recommending hostility—had to be held to the crudest strain of their militantism.[6] Also, unless Mao's progressivism was such as to encompass some doubt in dealing with capitalist countries, his decision ought to have gone against his ideological judgments and responded rationally to the situation.[7] These would be thought relevant arguments in any manifest speech, and will be thought so in this claim.[8]

Figure 2.2. Mao at Stalin's side on a ceremony arranged for Stalin's 71st birthday in Moscow in December 1949.

31

The truth is, that before the "lost chance" school could hope to make any impression, it should be expected to illustrate the "Ward Case." They do mention this example to show the arrest of officials from the United States in Manchuria: first, because they were radical pro-Soviet local Communists who acted of their own accord,[9] and secondly, because the impressions of Angus I. Ward, the Consul to China, were that the Mayor of Manchuria desired to be friendly in his relations with the United States—a sentiment that formed the basis of much of Ward's speaking positively of the Chinese—at the first opportunity with Ambassador Stuart and the Secretary of State, who were not personally capable of utilizing it.

It is one of the characteristic arguments of the "lost chance" school to accord to the fractious elements between Mao Zedong and Joseph Stalin the assumption that Odd Arne Westad is supposed to have ascribed to their odd communications from 1935 onward, when Mao consolidated his leadership with the CCP. For the apotheosis of camaraderie Westad has substituted that of business; and he calls everything business that he finds in their agenda.[10] The quality of an example is in some respects a strong illustration that it was conducive to the peace proposals initiated by the KMT. This is the case when the leader of the Soviet Union acted as the mediator, and "advised" Mao to accept the peace proposals through which they could most effectively negotiate with the KMT.[11] Mao, who refused to negotiate with the KMT, preferred, in this manner, a military solution.[12] Stalin, once suspected of seeking to prevent Mao's offensives north of the Yangzi River, became a source of contention among the masters of China, who bound themselves to one another for the rise of Chinese nationalism, which was more or less guaranteed by their collective skepticism toward the Communists of the USSR.[13]

Of What Sort of Critique the "Lost Chance" Thesis Is Susceptible?

And this question has come, and will it come gradually. It is but of all the rest of it, that historians have either attempted to criticize the theory, or been permitted, by newly released evidence at a conference in Beijing in 1986 that brought researchers from China and the United States together, to show to the public that China "had not been interested in friendship with the United States in 1949."[14] As yet, very few of them have shown that

China was willing to experience direct intervention from an imperialist country. Let us remember in what manner revolutions finally are achieved, which would have prevented their final victory of Communism in China; and we may form some faint conception under what interests Mao or other members of the CCP attempted to confuse, delay intervention, and stop aid to Chiang Kai-shek's forces.[15] The greatest test that Mao had set out for the United States—to show him that they would not pass, in stopping aid to the KMT and recognizing the People's Republic of China as an equal—was to instruct the Australian journalist, Michael Keon, not to deliver them any message from Washington as a reply to Zhou's friendly above-mentioned correspondence.[16] The essential part of how the United States had acted was mere sycophancy toward Mao. In the case of positive messages from the US, on the other hand, he suspected much of them would come with demanding terms and conditions. Therefore, Mao did not inculcate an interest beyond what was urged or recognized by him.[17]

But this was also the case with Ambassador Stuart's affairs. It often happens that the context of events is more significant. The Chinese had been growing more alarmed, since May 13, 1949, by the United States' military maneuvers in Qingdao, and more willing to confound them and reduce the possibility of a military engagement. Yet, in this case especially, whether there were such other ways can also be questioned concerning the real intentions of the Chinese in extending friendliness toward Stuart. The general opinion of Huang in his second meeting with Stuart is supposed to be, that the harassment and blockade at sea could have come from the United States. They might be supposed to think that the friendly gesture of the Communists was of all things the most deceptive to the United States; insomuch that they wanted to avoid confrontation with it—if not to reduce aid to the KMT. If the conversation with Stuart represented the real opinion of Huang in general, it would be seen that he wanted the United States to leave China alone, "that all the CCP wanted from the US was stoppage of aid and severance of relations with the KMT Government."[18]

It will be well to discuss the CCP's genuine intention through the particular arrest of the United States officials in Manchuria against whom suspicion of espionage on behalf of the KMT forces was directed; the arrests which the protests of Washington annexed to their release.[19] The "Ward Case," being the clue appointed by the "lost chance" clique for argumentation, the pro-Soviets at the local level and the Party Center which had little control over them, should be considered incorrect, in the sense that those who were in charge had ordered local Communists to report to the center; they were under the supposition that every action would have been instructed by the party, that they might have firm control over any foreign policy matter.[20] The CCP, however, both in this, and in all other incidents, preferred to realize its policy by "squeezing out" American and other Western diplomats in the "liberated zone"—but the Ward Case was the only case in which they had substantially persisted in confusing and irritating them so as to compel their departure from China.[21] Originally the CCP wanted to force the revolution without disturbance from the United States or others.[22]

For a long time, Steven M. Goldstein has believed ideology to be the underlying reason behind these incidents, and that there were no corresponding agreements with regard to the United States.[23] By the old ideological and historical conflicts of Socialism and capitalism, colonialism and liberation, the Chinese Communists did not trust capitalist countries; Chiang was literally regarded as the United States' "running dog," inasmuch as the takeover of China by Mao's archenemy was an alternative to a direct military intervention. Because the *Liberation Daily* published an article in April 1945 (reflective of the broader anti-capitalist tone of the time), the Chinese had supposed that all in China would have become a mirror image of Latin America in regard to the United States' monopoly over the region's economy—and they persistently held that this was its imperialist ambition.[24]

Meanwhile, the Soviet Union's model of "people's dictatorship" was the actual revolutionary path of Chinese Communism: much more so, as far as ideological adoption goes, than the evolutionary path so-called.[25] The CCP members maintained that the revolutionary imperative stops short of upholding treaties, debts, and covenants from previous governments, but it certainly extended to opposition to Western encroachment.[26] They could undertake no solution whatsoever but by driving—at least irritating—westerners out of the country. In this respect, Dean Acheson's remark to the British ambassador in Washington about the revolutionary path of Communism was notable in indicating the PRC's selective recognition of the obligations of the previous regimes: on March 5, 1949, for example, Mao stated that China should "refuse to recognize the legal status of any foreign diplomatic establishments and personnel of the Kuomintang period."[27] To a certain extent, imitation of the Soviet Union guaranteed their pro-Soviet and anti-Western orientation. Senior party members within the PRC wanted an analogous advantage by forcing "all Western interests and influence out of China."[28] Since a free-trade economy is incompatible with Communism, a Socialist generally prefers the dictatorship of the proletariat.[29]

On the Connection Between Revolution and Utility

What was it, then, which entirely tempered the ideological influences of foreign policy, and made it compatible with the statement that CCP leaders were not all ideological fanatics? Mere pragmatic means, though of great effect in short-term incidents, had much more use in achieving the long-term goals of the revolution; for their ideology only lasted while the domestic factor was present. The real nationwide factors were the pressure exerted by rank-and-file Communists against imperialist countries, in so far as Mao feared that having closer relations with the United States would make the Chinese Revolution lose its momentum, and the CCP's goal was sufficiently congenial with his to excite nationalistic sentiments amongst the people against imminent danger from "western imperialist encroachment."[30] The Ward Case demonstrates the patriotic mobilization of the people against foreign imperialism, whereas Mao's general fear of "imperialist representatives" in China concerned the Chinese bourgeoisie and intelligentsia, who saw Anglo-Saxon America as the "epitome of modern development"—towards each of which there was a need for anti-Western policies.[31]

Figure 2.3. John Leighton Stuart attended National Assembly of the Republic of China as the ambassador of the United States.

It is not true that in all recorded tensions between the Soviet Union and China, the former must have tended toward America; still less that the disagreement between Mao and Stalin must have strained their willingness to cooperate.[32] The most dominant aspect of voluntary association, Chen Jian observes, was the extensive telegraphic exchange in policy coordination since 1936; and it was found—or thought—necessary to plan secret missions, in sending out party members and advisers.[33] If the CCP dealt with Western officials as it did with the American ambassador, Stuart, Mao would have informed Moscow of the contact as if it were their personal concern.[34] Moreover, the contention between Mao and Stalin over the issue of a peace proposal by the KMT was resolved when Mao accepted Stalin's advice, and that Soviet aid was to be designated as the essential factor in helping the CCP win the civil war.[35] The two leaders agreed on this: the international proletarian revolution showed it to be necessary that the Soviet Union should lead the movement, or that the partnership should allow China to promote the revolution in the East. The Chinese Chairman wanted an alliance with the USSR, and even if the latter did not, it was almost always desirable that he should try all measures before attaining the goal of Socialism. It is true that the prevention of the United States from invading China depended on a military pact with the Soviet Union: one superpower must have been made their ally—even by provocation.[36]

General Conclusion

The real practical fault of the proponents of the "lost chance" thesis, to whomever may be given the historical authority, is that it treats the Chinese Communists as passive actors—as it even now does—who embraced Moscow in response to the actions of the United States. The mere fact that this view is usually American-centric will in most cases give the assumption of sincerity to the overtures of China; at least until they question the "Zhou *démarche*" and the "Ward Case," from which they will recognize, in the clearest manner, that the difference in their reasons was of ideological and pragmatic importance. Indeed, the assumption of "lost chance" pragmatism, either nationally or locally, and of decision-making by Chairman Mao, will not necessarily tell for much. Rather, this chapter has demonstrated how Mao used pragmatic means for the apprehension that the enemies of Communism in international politics (as was the United States in Asia) could not satisfactorily hinder the long-term goal of Socialism in China. Things also came to an issue of domestic opposition from the bourgeoisie on the one side, and solidarity with the Soviets on the other, except where the release of evidence altogether was swayed by political considerations at the time (such as the conference mentioned). Some may even question whether the very thing by which an amicable settlement of differences could become possible was the United States' will to stop aid to the KMT and become pro-Communist; as historians submit to a methodology, knowing full well there is a court of funders in the background, to whom they know they can be forced to obey. But to make the counterarguments parallel, we must consider that the evidence of the thesis of "lost chance" was, not to ordain the source, but to give persuasion always for the same country, like that of the United States. If so, their admission to it would be a grievous motive to induce people to agree to almost any arbitration in regard to non-Anglophone persons or states, and it would be just the same with the People's Republic of China.

ENDNOTES

[1]   Barbara W. Tuchman, "If Mao Had Come to Washington: An Essay in Alternatives," *Foreign Affairs* 51, no. 1 (October 1972), https://www. foreignaffairs.com/articles/china/if-mao-had-come-washington-nixon-tuchman; Warren I. Cohen, "Symposium: Rethinking the Lost Chance in China; Introduction: Was There a 'Lost Chance' in China?," *Diplomatic History* 21, no. 1 (Winter 1997): 71–75, https://www.jstor.org/stable/24913404.

[2]   Michael M. Sheng, "Chinese Communist Policy Toward the United States and the Myth of the 'Lost Chance' 1948–1950," *Modern Asian Studies* 28, no. 3 (July 1994): 475, 489, https://doi.org/10.1017/S0026749X00011835; Chen Jian, "The Myth of America's 'Lost Chance' in China: A Chinese Perspective in Light of New Evidence," *Diplomatic History* 21, no. 1 (Winter 1997): 79, https://www. jstor.org/stable/24913405; "The Ambassador in China (Stuart) to the Secretary of State," June 8, 1949, in *Foreign Relations of the United States, 1949*, vol. 8, *The Far East: China*, ed. Francis C. Prescott, Ralph R. Goodwin, Herbert A. Fine, and Velma Hastings Cassidy (Washington, DC: United States Government Printing Office, 1978), doc. 898, https://history.state.gov/historicaldocuments/frus1949v08/d898.

[3]   Sheng, "Chinese Communist Policy Toward the United States and the Myth of the 'Lost Chance' 1948–1950," 491; Michael M. Sheng, "America's Lost Chance in China? A Reappraisal of Chinese Communist Policy Toward the United States before 1945," *Australian Journal of Chinese Affairs* 29 (January 1993): 135–157, https://doi.org/10.2307/2949955.

[4]   "The Consul General at Peiping (Clubb) to the Secretary of State," June 2, 1949, in *Foreign Relations of the United States, 1949*, vol. 9, *The Far East: China*, ed. Francis C. Prescott, Herbert A. Fine, and Velma Hastings Cassidy (Washington, DC: United States Government Printing Office, 1974), doc. 884, https://history.state.gov/historicaldocuments/frus1949v09/d884.

[5]   Cohen, "Symposium," 74; Sheng, "Chinese Communist Policy Toward the United States and the Myth of the 'Lost Chance' 1948–1950," 475; Tuchman, "If Mao Had Come to Washington."

[6]   "The Consul General at Peiping (Clubb) to the Secretary of State," June 1, 1949, in *Foreign Relations of the United States, 1949*, vol. 8, *The Far East: China*, ed. Francis C. Prescott, Ralph R. Goodwin, Herbert A. Fine, and Velma Hastings Cassidy (Washington, DC: United States Government Printing Office, 1978), doc. 425, https://history.state.gov/historicaldocuments/frus1949v08/d425; "Cable, Liu Shaoqi to Mao Zedong," July 18, 1949, Wilson Center Digital Archive, *Jianguo yilai Liu Shaoqi wengao* [Liu Shaoqi's manuscripts since the founding of the PRC], vol. 1, trans. David Wolff (Beijing: Zhongyang wenxian chubanshe, 2005), 30–37, https://digitalarchive.wilsoncenter.org/

document/113439.

[7] Sheng, "America's Lost Chance in China?," 135–157.

[8] Cohen, "Symposium," 73; Sheng, "Chinese Communist Policy Toward the United States and the Myth of the 'Lost Chance' 1948–1950," 493.

[9] Sheng, "Chinese Communist Policy Toward the United States and the Myth of the 'Lost Chance' 1948–1950," 479.

[10] Sheng, "America's Lost Chance in China?," 137; Odd Arne Westad, "Unwrapping the Stalin-Mao Talks: Setting the Record Straight," *Cold War International History Project Bulletin*, no. 6–7 (Winter 1995/1996): 23–24, https://www.wilsoncenter.org/sites/default/files/media/documents/publication/CWIHP_Bulletin_6-7.pdf.

[11] "Cable, Filippov [Stalin] to Cde. Mao Zedong," January 14, 1949, Wilson Center Digital Archive, Archive of the President of the Russian Federation (APRF), f. 45, op. 1, d. 330, ll. 110–113; Russian State Archive of Socio-Political History (RGASPI), f. 558, op. 11, d. 330, ll. 0110–0113, contributed by Sergey Radchenko, https://digitalarchive.wilsoncenter.org/document/116969; "Ciphered Telegrams No. 50450, 50470, and 50490, Terebin to Kuznetsov, Transmitting a Message from Mao Zedong to Filippov [Stalin]," January 13, 1949, Wilson Center Digital Archive, Archive of the President of the Russian Federation (APRF), f. 45, op. 1, d. 330; Russian State Archive of Socio-Political History (RGASPI), f. 558, op. 11, d. 330, ll. 0100, 0101–0102, 0103, contributed by Sergey Radchenko, https://digitalarchive.wilsoncenter.org/document/112663.

[12] "Cable, Stalin to Mao Zedong, Nanjing Peace Proposal," January 10, 1949, Wilson Center Digital Archive, Archive of the President of the Russian Federation (APRF), f. 45, op. 1, d. 330, ll. 95–96, https://digitalarchive.wilsoncenter.org/document/112659; Odd Arne Westad, "Rivals and Allies: Stalin, Mao, and the Chinese Civil War, January 1949," *Cold War International History Project Bulletin*, no. 6–7 (Winter 1995/1996): 7, https://www.wilsoncenter.org/sites/default/files/media/documents/publication/CWIHP_Bulletin_6-7.pdf; Mao Tse-tung, "Farewell, Leighton Stuart!," in *Selected Works of Mao Tse-tung*, vol. 4, *The Third Revolutionary Period* (Peking: Foreign Languages Press, 1961), 433–440, https://www.marxists.org/reference/archive/mao/selected-works/volume-4/mswv4_67.htm.

[13] Westad, "Rivals and Allies," 7; Westad, "Unwrapping the Stalin-Mao Talks," 23; Tuchman, "If Mao Had Come to Washington."

[14] Cohen, "Symposium," 74.

[15] Sheng, "Chinese Communist Policy Toward the United States and the Myth of the 'Lost Chance' 1948–1950," 486; Sheng, "America's Lost Chance in China?," 136.

[16] Sheng, "Chinese Communist Policy Toward the United States and the Myth of the 'Lost Chance' 1948–1950," 491; Jian, "The Myth of America's 'Lost Chance' in China," 81.

[17] Mao, "Farewell, Leighton Stuart!"

[18] Sheng, "Chinese Communist Policy Toward the United States and the Myth of the 'Lost Chance' 1948–1950," 490.

[19]   Sheng, "Chinese Communist Policy Toward the United States and the Myth of the 'Lost Chance' 1948–1950," 476; Jian, "The Myth of America's 'Lost Chance' in China," 77–78.

[20]   Sheng, "Chinese Communist Policy Toward the United States and the Myth of the 'Lost Chance' 1948–1950," 478–479.

[21]   Jian, "The Myth of America's 'Lost Chance' in China," 77.

[22]   Sheng, "Chinese Communist Policy Toward the United States and the Myth of the 'Lost Chance' 1948–1950," 477, 482, 484.

[23]   Sheng, "Chinese Communist Policy Toward the United States and the Myth of the 'Lost Chance' 1948–1950," 486.

[24]   Sheng, "Chinese Communist Policy Toward the United States and the Myth of the 'Lost Chance' 1948–1950," 488, 493.

[25]   Sheng, "Chinese Communist Policy Toward the United States and the Myth of the 'Lost Chance' 1948–1950," 497; Odd Arne Westad, "Losses, Chances, and Myths: The United States and the Creation of the Sino-Soviet Alliance, 1945–1950," *Diplomatic History* 21, no. 1 (Winter 1997): 114, https://www.jstor.org/stable/24913408.

[26]   Sheng, "Chinese Communist Policy Toward the United States and the Myth of the 'Lost Chance' 1948–1950," 477, 481.

[27]   Sheng, "Chinese Communist Policy Toward the United States and the Myth of the 'Lost Chance' 1948–1950," 482, 485.

[28]   Sheng, "Chinese Communist Policy Toward the United States and the Myth of the 'Lost Chance' 1948–1950," 477–478.

[29]   Sheng, "Chinese Communist Policy Toward the United States and the Myth of the 'Lost Chance' 1948–1950," 494.

[30]   Westad, "Losses, Chances, and Myths," 115; Sheng, "Chinese Communist Policy Toward the United States and the Myth of the 'Lost Chance' 1948–1950," 498.

[31]   Westad, "Losses, Chances, and Myths," 115; Sheng, "Chinese Communist Policy Toward the United States and the Myth of the 'Lost Chance' 1948–1950," 484.

[32]   Jian, "The Myth of America's 'Lost Chance' in China," 82.

[33]   Sheng, "America's Lost Chance in China?," 137; Jian, "The Myth of America's 'Lost Chance' in China," 82–83.

[34]   Jian, "The Myth of America's 'Lost Chance' in China," 83; "Cable, Kovalev to Stalin, Report on the 22 May 1949 CCP CC Politburo Discussion," May 23, 1949, Wilson Center Digital Archive, Archive of the President of the Russian Federation (APRF), f. 45, op. 1, d. 331, ll. 66–69; Russian State Archive of Socio-Political History (RGASPI), f. 558, op. 11, d. 331, ll. 0066–0069, reprinted in Andrei Ledovskii, Raisa Mirovitskaia, and Vladimir Miasnikov, *Sovetsko-Kitaiskie Otnosheniia*, vol. 5, bk. 2, 1946–February 1950, trans. Sergey Radchenko (Moscow: Pamiatniki Istoricheskoi Mysli, 2005), 132–134, https://digitalarchive.wilsoncenter.org/document/113365; "Report, Kovalev to Stalin," December 24, 1949, Wilson Center Digital Archive, Archive of the

President of the Russian Federation (APRF), f. 3, op. 65, d. 584, ll. 123–144, reprinted in Andrei Ledovskii, Raisa Mirovitskaia, and Vladimir Miasnikov, *Sovetsko-Kitaiskie Otnosheniia*, vol. 5, bk. 2, 1946–February 1950, trans. Sergey Radchenko (Moscow: Pamiatniki Istoricheskoi Mysli, 2005), 234–243, https:// digitalarchive.wilsoncenter.org/document/113441.

[35]   Jian, "The Myth of America's 'Lost Chance' in China," 83.

[36]   Sheng, "Chinese Communist Policy Toward the United States and the Myth of the 'Lost Chance' 1948–1950," 477; Westad, "Losses, Chances, and Myths," 114.

CHAPTER III

> A blackened performance space is energized through the song
> "Flying Down to Rio" as originally sung by Fred Astaire and
> interpreted by Ginger Rogers through her dancing. Images
> of King Kong fighting biplanes at the top of the Empire State
> Building are projected on to a blackened backdrop. When
> this tune is halfway through the houselights go up and the
> DP [Dancing Pilot] waltzes on to the stage dressed as a World
> War One pilot. She is quickly followed by two silver angels
> who place a flip chart stage right, alongside marker pens and
> voting cards.
>
> —David William Parry, *Women in Mayhem*

In *The War in the Air: And Particularly How Mr. Bert Smallways Fared
While It Lasted*, Mr. Herbert George Wells foresaw then the destruction
of modern civilization without the use of land and sea forces.[1] Without
troubling ourselves about the thread of the plot, the father of science fiction's
tale portrayed the fantastic terrors of indiscriminate bomber aircraft impressed
on the feelings of those who read it.[2] I have little doubt that his ideas on the
superiority of airpower had a magnetic influence over the minds of at least
two generations later; many were well-nigh persuaded to believe the force
of airpower alone could put an end at once to each sound of war and woe.
Indeed, musing over the events of various operations in the late twentieth
century, "air power has emerged as the preferred instrument of force by the
West."[3]

Figure 3.1. A Zeppelin passenger ship.

Others, however, could not forebear remonstrating strongly against this innovation, declaring that their aircraft, aircrew, and air cargo, were not enough to achieve singly a fatal and a bloody victory. Such was the generally received belief of its advantages that the great powers in the two world wars and developed countries within these thirty or forty years, gave much attention to that implement of war. The British Royal Air Force (RAF) itself, by precept and example, regards air power as "the ability to project power from the air and space to influence the behavior of people or the course of events."[4] Be it so, I do not intend to jump into the plane and presently resume the various and numerous definitions applied to air power. But, as matters stand, I wonder whether air power can contend with the winds of necessity and/or the calms of sufficiency (upon the point of falling prey to "Flying Down to Rio," namely the favorite tune of the Dancing Pilot in the Rev. Parry's *Women in Mayhem: Or Three Nonsensical Pranks*).[5]

For this purpose, I begin to explain the exertions dashed against the necessity or sufficiency of airpower. Then come the reasons to fear modern military aircraft, secured as they are by the spirit of surgeonship that seized on Daedalus when he molded into symmetry a pair of wings for Icarus; and next, I will but find out whether the reputation of airpower is founded in reality, by uncoiling the carefully arranged cordage of former studies, in order to ascertain the limitations of airpower. In this process of reasoning, I will take under my consideration some general cases that passed between the fatal morning which succeeded the declaration of war at midnight on August 3/4, 1914, and the day when the Dayton Agreement was signed in Paris, on December 14, 1995, to end the Bosnian War. It is scarce necessary to add, that though the object of my journalistic researches is the place of airpower in modern warfare, I give way to things past because they determine things future, and we know that all views of the practice of airpower in the present day are shaped by the dim specters through which superior officers of the air force kept sight of any failure or success.

Figure 3.2. The Fall of Icarus.

Olympian Fragments

In short, it is conjectured that airpower is curtailed by the way in which it can "only deliver a fraction of the firepower available to artillery," so that there is nothing save the constant pressure of force that can be said to approach the banquet of Nike, the old goddess of victory.[6] To this objurgation, Colin McInnes adds the corroborating demonstration of an example: "NATO [North Atlantic Treaty Organization] air strikes were unable to prevent Serb ethnic cleansing in Kosovo in part because they lacked the firepower."[7] Moreover, it is now held, that though airpower may cause the necessary

45

preparations "for land power, and can perhaps deny the use of territory to an enemy," it cannot take and occupy territories.[8] This is more especially true of those mortal emergencies, such as might be fetched by the devil, "if territory is to be (re)gained and then held."[9] Therefore, although airpower may not be sufficient unassisted, yet, on the whole, it may be necessary. At length McInnes, who comprehends the nature of the situation, resumes his discourse with emphasis:

> [I]n his study of airpower in World War II, Richard Overy concluded that, despite the pre-war predictions, "aircraft did not replace navies and armies ... successful warfare still depended upon the movement of armies to occupy land and the movement of ships to provide supplies and men." Airpower made the use of sea and land power more effective, and in some theatres, it was indispensable. But it was not sufficient to secure victory and operated in support of, or in harness with, other forms of military power.[10]

It was, indeed, during the First World War that airpower was much used as a kind of "tactical support, using ground-attack aircraft or bombers to break up enemy attacks, destroy artillery, disrupt reinforcement of the battlefield, and bomb or strafe rear communications and supply depots."[11] Thus, if the reader will pardon one or two illustrations: "in November 1917 at Cambrai aircraft helped to ease the path of British tanks whose attack threatened to collapse under accurate German artillery fire."[12] And in the other,

> The Polish campaign set the pattern of tactical air power. Aircraft gave surface forces much greater flexibility and striking power, but only where they were concentrated together, as German air forces were, into large air fleets, and where communication between air and ground forces was technically sophisticated enough to co-ordinate air and ground attacks and to call up air assistance in minutes.[13]

By far, the incidents that I have introduced in the chapter appear to give a quick indication of the necessity of airpower in military operations. But perhaps, like the *ennui* of the most protracted morning meal, this is not enough, and I must needs provide the positive conviction, that airpower is sufficient to gain the victory which might be expected.

Birds of Prey

Here and there one can readily hear the exaggerated words, uttered with the air of the cloud-compeller Jupiter himself, that aerial supremacy has revolutionized war and can now finish conflicts in a matter of days.[14] General Giulio Douhet took his place amongst others in this sport, and wrote in his *The Command of the Air* that air power alone could determine the outcome of all conflicts.[15] This defense serves as a preface to the presentation of a punch-bowl of notable examples—of these the reader may be acquainted with the following specimen: "in the Battle of the Coral Sea and the Battle of Midway, Japanese expansion in the Pacific was ended by American naval aviators who succeeded with just ten bomb hits in sinking all four Japanese aircraft-carriers committed to the conflict. In neither battle was a shot fired by a naval gun; the outcome was decided by aircraft."[16] It is no wonder that airpower is considered a tool with which underbred political puppets, as well as their condescending paymasters in the defense industry (in the United States and allied nations), coerce weak countries.[17] It is therefore not surprising to ejaculate, "Stanley Baldwin's prophecy has now come true. Bombers almost always do get through, owing to doctrinal and technological developments that allow the best air forces to suppress all but the very best air defence systems."[18] Frequently, also, did it happen, that "bombers and missiles now strike their targets with a consistency that was scarcely imaginable in earlier times."[19]

Besides this, recent anecdotes of its success have gained airpower command and respect: "There are certain dates in the history of warfare that mark real turning points. Now there is a new turning point to fix on the calendar: June 3, 1999, when the capitulation of President Milosevic proved that a war can be won by airpower alone . . . the air forces have won a triumph, are entitled to every plaudit they will receive and can look forward to enjoying a transformed status in the strategic community, one they have earned by their single-handed efforts."[20] To give some sense of airpower's merits, in the light of NATO's bombing campaign against the Federal Republic of Yugoslavia during the Kosovo War, "after 78 days of bombing the Serb leadership gave way, without NATO having to use ground troops," a result that followed the commanding manner of Operation Deliberate Force in which the air forces coerced the leaders of Republika Srpska in the Republic of Bosnia and Herzegovina.[21] Benjamin Lambeth mentions similar instances, particularly that of Operation Desert Storm in 1991, when the Gulf War, "marked, for many, the final emergence of airpower as the dominant instrument of combat power." Airpower did not simply assist in securing victory; it determined the outcome of the military struggle. Despite the rhetoric of joint operations, for airpower advocates the Gulf War demonstrated a new military reality: that the tables had been turned and land and sea power now supported airpower.[22]

Let us debate this further, and we find, *volens nolens*—"Because air power can strike at key political and economic targets directly, . . . it can bring sufficient pressures upon an enemy leadership to coerce them into acceding to the West's demands without extensive recourse to sea and land power."[23] This peculiarity, of course, arises from the technological innovations and the "transformed nature of war whereby the target is no longer the state or the people, but the enemy leadership," which is "arguably a much easier target on which to bring coercive pressure to bear via air power."[24] Such arguments and examples, therefore, advocate airpower as a sufficient military force. To a bald, sunburnt spectator—like the drunken old "Ballsbig" in Parry's unpublished play, set in Benidorm—these evident marks of success or dexterity, at first sight, may be liable to some deception.

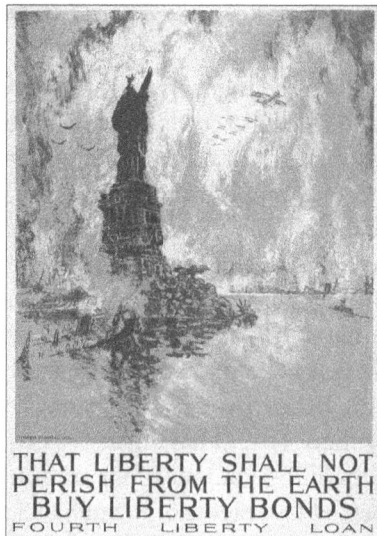

THAT LIBERTY SHALL NOT
PERISH FROM THE EARTH
BUY LIBERTY BONDS
FOURTH   LIBERTY   LOAN

Figure 3.3. This poster depicts the dire consequences of a German victory, showing the Statue of Liberty engulfed in flames with German bombers overhead.

Air power also has its demoralizing effect on the mental perturbation of trained soldiers, as was remarkably visible during the First and Second World Wars: "Against even seasoned troops air attack initially created panic quite out of proportion to the actual threat."[25] On the latter occasion in particular, the leading theorists of strategic bombing took much notice of "the success of bombing in the Pacific War, where city attacks brought Japan to the point of surrender without the need for costly assault on the Japanese home islands."[26] Overy produces a nod as well as a wink—elsewhere in place, and likewise in time—parallel to one in the Pacific theater: "In 1917, armed with the Gotha IV bomber, the German high command ordered bomb attacks on British cities to 'destroy the morale of the British people' and take Britain out of the war."[27]

The *RAF War Manual*, published in 1936, touched on a leaden-colored sky, obscured by a burst of rain of a coarse dark-colored iron-stone, so molded for the deeds of war and slaughter, which dropped on the blackened and scorched creatures of flesh and blood down below, imagined boldly that "the bomb is the chief weapon of an air force."[28] "The main objective of bombing," says the erudite Overy, "was to destroy the enemy's capacity to make war by destroying the economy and moral reserves that sustained it."[29] Then with that, Overy adds, insisting on the particulars of the commonly received promise of flying vessels: "The bomber fleet, whose progress to its target was widely regarded as unstoppable in the 1920s, became the central instrument in British air theory, capable, it was argued, of deciding the outcome of a war on its own."[30] And it would not be saying, perhaps, too much, to aver, that as nuclear weapons are "delivered by aircraft or missiles, . . . it is easy to believe that their detonations, if sufficiently numerous, will render the activities of armies and navies inconsequential."[31] It is nevertheless to be presumed, that a bomber was well "regarded as the key instrument in the attack on the enemy home front in any conflict which did not involve atomic weapons."[32] This naturally substitutes air strikes for atomic bombs, which we suppose to be preeminently powerful—or pre-eminently wicked!

Reluctance to Save Falling Pilots

Having presented a picture of airpower in our sight, I think it is time to closely reconnoiter the full weight of airpower, in order to procure intelligence respecting its weaknesses, and, in theory at least, to know that it is of itself sufficient to gain the victory. Certain it is, it will be observed by historians, that the general balance of the advantages afforded by airpower can scarcely be placed in the front rank of the annals of history, in modern days, of military victory and glory.

And I may say, literally as well as figuratively, that the flying choosers of the slain in 1917 produced a negligible strategic effect on the British Empire, from the cognizance of which came, like an eagle that sallied from his cliff, with ire in his eye, and haste in his wing, but presently found himself compelled to close his wounded sails before his precipitate retreat, the resolution to "return to battlefront priorities."[33] With such occasions in view, it is still more extraordinary: "A post-war bombing survey conducted by American intelligence showed that bombing had not halted German production, nor had it produced insupportable demoralization."[34] For, as sure as that nature has implanted the freedom of will within our hollow breast, so surely is "the possibility that such attacks will inspire an escalatory response from the other side . . . The aim of violence in war is always to break the enemy's will. Yet it may equally well harden his heart, stiffen his spine, and stimulate his imagination instead."[35] This point being established, it is worth while saying, the power of utter destruction, with which bombers were armed, had hitherto been denied by mechanical bluntness. So far as could be guessed, it was soon reported that institutional interests were disposed "to compromise objective analysis."[36]

Perhaps some, even of the better class, as Sir Arthur "Bomber" Harris himself, would be a little nettled by the way in which the echoes of area bombing in the course of the Second World War, even when it seemed the only means of elevating triumph, "aroused deep moral concerns after the war. Objections to bombing civilians were muted before 1945, but the evidence of civilian casualties (over a million in Germany and Japan together), and the growing realization that the RAF had deliberately pursued attacks on whole urban targets, rather than just factories, provoked a backlash against bombing in the western states."[37] After these details, it may be easily imagined, that though bombing rendered it difficult for the German Reich to expand its war efforts, yet the Thousand-Year Reich on whom they commenced a sweeping attack by air could not be prevailed upon to display a white flag.[38] The surrender happened "through the physical occupation of Germany by Allied armies."[39]

To be plain, just as they compared the supposed capabilities of the air force, at all events, to deliver a "knock-out blow," Overy remarks, comprehending the situation, "most professional soldiers, sailors, and even airmen were sceptical of air power. They did not regard aircraft as war winners on their own, and indeed sought to make aviation a subordinate service, assisting, but not supplanting, armies and navies."[40] And at least, their opinions with respect to the attributes of airpower were the same: "war in the air is difficult, dangerous, and disappointing, just like war everywhere else."[41] They mentioned similar instances, particularly of aerial warfare in the Great War, which "only produced demonstrable military advantage when used in conjunction with ground forces, or to interrupt the immediate reinforcement of the battlefront."[42] It was not therefore surprising that "the view of air power as auxiliary was more widespread in the inter-war years than belief in the knock-out blow."[43]

Besides, it is easy to criticize the ineffective discharge of such operations as those of the United States Air Force (USAF), the most powerful of air forces, has engaged, judging by the rate at which it has failed them. In the days of Tricky Dicky— somewhat fragrant with the smell of napalm at morning or when evening was about to fall—"Persistent losses of B52 bombers in attacks on the North were expensive in men and equipment, but also called into question the whole credibility of the bombing campaign. When President [Richard] Nixon finally suspended bomb attacks in 1973 air power had gained nothing decisive. Two years later the North Vietnamese triumphed."[44]

At other times, especially when air defense had perceptibly begun to ascend the technological acclivity, there was an air of inconsequence about aerial bombing.[45] Certainly, in the perusal of World War II history, to which our attention has frequently turned, we have occasion to acknowledge, that "the development of radar permitted the early warning of air attack; anti-aircraft batteries and civil defence preparations reduced the risk to urban populations."[46] We are obliged to confess, then, that air superiority was necessary for success; the more obviously, to be sure, when this precondition was united with the wild chorus of their attack upon "Ten German Bombers."[47]

Lastly, contrary to what seems, at first view, to be a simple scheme for success, the cases already mentioned (the Kosovo War, etc.) were not simple and uniform incidents, they being each attended with its own peculiar state of the atmosphere, among certain other conflicting causes. Hence, it is the general opinion that,

> Operation Deliberate Force also included substantial artillery attacks from British and French forces on Mount Igman while the mounting Bosnian government and Croat ground offensive also placed considerable pressures on the Serbs. In Kosovo, air power was only one of a number of

pressures being exerted on the Serb leadership: the threat of a NATO ground offensive was growing, the Russians offered no support to Belgrade, KLP [Kosovo Liberation Army] operations in Kosovo were increasing and Milosevic had been indicted on war crimes charges.[48]

So, without further addition, McInnes concludes: "Arguing that air power alone determined the successful outcome of both Operation Deliberate Force and Operation Allied Force therefore appears problematic, though its key role in both is suggestive."[49]

The Pilot's Conclusion

In brief, I have ventured to throw the light of the dawning upon the force and situation of airpower to attain success in military operations and diplomacy, without observing the apparition of any other recommendable influence. The half-buried ruins described in this chapter should not be supposed universal; and having seen what effect airpower might have had upon the current of events, in which the entire ranges of the *Ultima Thule* of our dusky history, that stretched through the environs and outworks of the period betwixt 1914 and 1995, we have been favored with a distant prospect—concealed by a great mass of red clouds upon the horizon, in some vision glimpsed through our imaginative spy-glass—of what was said to be aerial operations, and have had opportunity to extract from the remotest recesses of independent and joint operations, amidst disjointed metals, two principal points; first, that air power is most effective in joint operations such as were sanctioned by the Wehrmacht to invade the Republic of Poland; and next, that in spite of the remarkable and rapid success of aerial warfare, which the Pacific War, the Kosovo War, the Bosnian War seemed to exhibit, we cannot avoid saying they were isolated or unlikely episodes sequestered by the extremity of their situation, probably in consequence of the favorable winds of other agitating determinants which bore them forward to the verge of an imminent victory. These conclusions, on the whole, are such as might open the discourse thus: air power itself alone can be quite sufficient to win against a whole circle of opponents for short term operational gains, but it is not likely to land strategic gains without the assistance of the sails of navies and the marches of armies. That air power is necessary but not sufficient is, therefore, in practice more attractive than the bold and daring tales chanted concerning the wonders of airplanes—or dragons told in the energetic rime of the ancient skalds!

ENDNOTES

[1] H. G. Wells, *The War in the Air* (London, 1908; Project Gutenberg, 2024), https://www.gutenberg.org/files/780/780-h/780-h.htm.

[2] Wells, *The War in the Air.*

[3] Colin McInnes, "Fatal Attraction? Air Power and the West," *Contemporary Security Policy* 22, no. 3 (2001): 28, https://doi.org/10.1080/135323605123313911 218.

[4] Centre for Air Power Studies, *AP 3000: British Air and Space Power Doctrine*, 4th ed. (Norwich: Her Majesty's Stationery Office, 2009), 7.

[5] David William Parry, *Women in Mayhem: Or Three Nonsensical Pranks* (Melbourne: Manticore Press, 2024), 9.

[6] McInnes, "Fatal Attraction?," 45–46.

[7] McInnes, "Fatal Attraction?," 46.

[8] McInnes, "Fatal Attraction?," 46.

[9] McInnes, "Fatal Attraction?," 46.

[10] Colin McInnes, *Spectator-Sport War: The West and Contemporary Conflict* (London: Lynne Rienner, 2002), 105.

[11] Richard Overy, "Air Warfare," in *The Oxford History of Modern War*, ed. Charles Townshend (Oxford: Oxford University Press, 2005), 264.

[12] Overy, "Air Warfare," 265.

[13] Overy, "Air Warfare," 270.

[14] Overy, "Air Warfare," 266.

[15] Giulio Douhet, *The Command of the Air*, trans. Dino Ferrari (Washington, DC: Office of Air Force History, 1983).

[16] Overy, "Air Warfare," 272.

[17] Daniel Moran, "Geography and Strategy," in *Strategy in the Contemporary World: An Introduction to Strategic Studies*, 3rd ed., ed. John Baylis, James J. Wirtz, and Colin S. Gray (Oxford: Oxford University Press, 2010), 135.

[18] Moran, "Geography and Strategy," 135.

[19] Moran, "Geography and Strategy," 135.

[20] McInnes, "Fatal Attraction?," 28.

[21] McInnes, "Fatal Attraction?," 45.

[22] McInnes, *Spectator-Sport War*, 105.

[23] McInnes, "Fatal Attraction?," 44–45.

[24] McInnes, "Fatal Attraction?," 45.

25   Overy, "Air Warfare," 265.

26   Overy, "Air Warfare," 276.

27   Overy, "Air Warfare," 265.

28   Overy, "Air Warfare," 267.

29   Overy, "Air Warfare," 267.

30   Overy, "Air Warfare," 267.

31   Moran, "Geography and Strategy," 135.

32   Overy, "Air Warfare," 276.

33   Overy, "Air Warfare," 265.

34   Overy, "Air Warfare," 276.

35   Moran, "Geography and Strategy," 135.

36   Moran, "Geography and Strategy," 134.

37   Overy, "Air Warfare," 276.

38   Overy, "Air Warfare," 275.

39   Overy, "Air Warfare," 275.

40   Overy, "Air Warfare," 266.

41   Moran, "Geography and Strategy," 134.

42   Overy, "Air Warfare," 267.

43   Overy, "Air Warfare," 266.

44   Overy, "Air Warfare," 277.

45   Overy, "Air Warfare," 269.

46   Overy, "Air Warfare," 269.

47   Overy, "Air Warfare," 274.

48   McInnes, "Fatal Attraction?," 45.

49   McInnes, "Fatal Attraction?," 45.

PART II

GLOBAL POLITICS WORKING AGAINST RATIONAL BOUNDARIES

CHAPTER IV

DO STATES FORM A SOCIETY? SKETCHES OF HEDLEY BULL'S IDEA OF *THE ANARCHICAL SOCIETY*

This chapter is intended merely as a brief abstract of the extent to which states form a society. This can be done by viewing the ideological and practical grounds of the concept of the "anarchical society" introduced by Hedley Bull. Indeed, history or tradition, being interrogated, tells us of three distinct schools of thought in international relations, on the one side; on the other, practical arguments. According to Martin Wight, the three main belief systems are occupied by the Hobbesian or realist tradition, the Kantian or revolutionist tradition, and the Grotian or internationalist tradition;[1] the practical arguments are connected with historical records as well as the progress of globalization.

The prescient eye of Bull saw states forming the basic unit of international relations, with their government and sovereignty over a territory and population.[2] Bull suspected, "A system of states (or international system) is formed when two or more states have sufficient contact between them, and have sufficient impact on one another's decisions, to cause them to behave . . . as parts of a whole."[3] Or rather, they are sufficiently aware of the unity of their interests and values, so as to form a society, one which they consider "to be bound by a common set of rules in their relations with one another, and share in the working of common institutions."[4] In other words, it is "any association of distinct political communities that accept some common values, rules, and institutions."[5] In the proper sense, the whole is founded upon the "principles of sovereignty and non-intervention, and the institutions of diplomacy, the balance of power, and international law."[6] But, above all, this system of international relations is comparatively free from the bounds of higher authority, and does not present an inextricable chaos to those around it.

Figure 4.1. The headquarters of the United Nations (UN) seen from the gates of the Palace of Nations, in Geneva.

Against the Society of States

We have mentioned three distinct political theories of international relations. The Hobbesians describe international politics as a "state of war of all against all, an arena of struggle in which each state is pitted against every other."[7] In this condition, the occasion of quarrel between two or more states is recognized as a "zero-sum game," and totally excluding the manifest interests of the different states.[8] It is with this view that war might be said to form the inevitable course of international affairs. On the contrary, peace is considered a probable period of recovery to prepare the state for subsequent wars.[9] In this point of view, the nation would be able "to pursue its goals in relation to other states without moral or legal restrictions of any kind."[10] In fact, the "rules of prudence or expediency" govern the conduct of states with each other.[11] The history of the two world wars illustrates this propensity. In another example, the eventful struggle betwixt the Soviet Union and the United States occurred in spite of the presence of international organizations like the European Union or the United Nations, which were regarded as symbols of international society; for there was no "Supreme Authority" that could keep them in awe.[12] This conduct on the part of states is like that of individuals in mortal conflict, because no power can induce them to fear.[13] Therefore, a society of states cannot exist unless an authority managed the relationship between any two states.

The Kantians see international politics as a community composed potentially of all humans.[14] In this tradition, the trans-national unity of interest of any two individuals is deemed the fundamental principle on which international politics should be established.[15] This system, under which foreign disputes between states seem to be "superficial or transient," renders necessary the moral imperative to overthrow and replace the intercourse of international politics, or even the active cooperation of countries, with a cosmopolitan society.[16] There exists also a curious picture of the progress of society, evincing a similar event in history, presented by Ruhollah Khomeini (the first supreme leader of the Islamic Republic of Iran), that "the relations between nations should be based on spiritual grounds."[17] Not only did Khomeini look at "earthly governments" as illegitimate, but he affirmed that, "the state itself and the concept of nationality were equally invalid";[18] at any rate, the division of Muslims follows "unnatural territorial boundaries."[19] We are led, therefore, to believe that the society of states is difficult to conceive.

Figure 4.2. Dutch lawyer and statesman Hugo de Groot, also known as Hugo Grotius.

Still, it must be observed, that as globalization advances, and the hegemony of the United States, global poverty, climate change, anti-Westernism, and state failure extend beyond the frontiers of neighboring states, the theory of a "sovereignty-based international society" is gradually undermined.[20] Thus, for the first time, it can be proposed seriously that, globalization is imposing its own laws upon the international community. In short, it is not too much to say, that in the course of transnational corporations, advancing communication technologies, shared values and cultures, globalization threatens the boundaries of states, and encourages the project of a global "super-government" that, after all, renders it impossible to devise a society of states. Thus, globalization acts as a barrier against the development of international society.

The advocates of the establishment of a society of states are accused of legitimizing "an oppressive and exploitative colonial order" justified by the "standard of civilization" that, in English and European imperialist history, seized the foreign lands of the Americas, Africa and Australasia, and unequally treated nations like China and the Ottoman Empire.[21] In the proper sense, the ordinary discourse on the character of international society disguises its real object of extending the power and the privileges of one society over every other society.

Enthusiasm for the Society of States

The composition of the society of states is much more favorable to the Grotian or internationalist tradition, which, being moderate in its views, seeks to harbor the opinion that international politics takes place within the precincts of international society.[22] This doctrine informs us that states are not actively engaged in constant war with each other, as realists expect, but are limited by the common bounds of existing rules and institutions. Bull wrote, "The Grotian prescription for international conduct is that all states, in their dealings with one another, are bound by the rules and institutions of the society they form."[23] In stern opposition to the admirers of the Hobbesian faction, who insist that states are overcome by cold considerations of prudence and expediency, stand two imperatives recommended by the enlightened members of the Grotian faction—morality and law, namely—equally resolved to urge the co-operation and co-existence of societies, without having recourse to a "universal community of mankind."[24] The European Union, from the beginning, has been an example of such an assembly of societies. In like manner, in the earlier days of the twenty-first century, all the members of the United Nations approved of a "global covenant," as Robert Jackson termed it, now governed upon the genuine principles of non-intervention, independence, and, generally, "the sanctity, integrity and inviolability of all existing states, regardless of their level of development, form of government, political ideology, pattern of culture or any other domestic characteristic or condition."[25] This decisive step towards the ends of peace and order followed, of course, the decolonization of the colonies after the Second World War, while the popularity of the "European model of international society" increased without.[26] It must also be allowed, that although the whole basis of the most perfect international society was intended to exhibit the relations of the finest European nations, this association could refer to political ties in the four quarters of the globe; in fact, the three divisions of society are modern, traditional, and primitive, which almost resembles James Lorimer's distinction betwixt "civilized humanity, barbarous humanity and savage humanity."[27] So said, in this section I have endeavored to sum up the general views of the Grotianists or the English School.

Reflections

Those who look to the assertion that states cannot proceed to form a society, where there is no authority, ought to doubt whether it was not too hastily concluded. For though, on the one hand, it is to be supposed, that the Hobbesian state of existence permitted "no industry, agriculture, navigation, trade or other refinements of living because the strength and invention of men is absorbed in providing security against one another";[28] yet, on the other hand, it must be admitted, that the absence of a super-Leviathan does not stop the "international economic interdependence" of countries, whereas the increase of security against foreign invaders and internal dissension tends to facilitate the economic improvement of borders.[29] The Hobbesian project is further weakened by the sense that morality in the arena of international relations, and especially in the system of societies that arose out of Europe and so widely spread into nations outside the Continent, has "always held a central place" in principle and practice.[30]

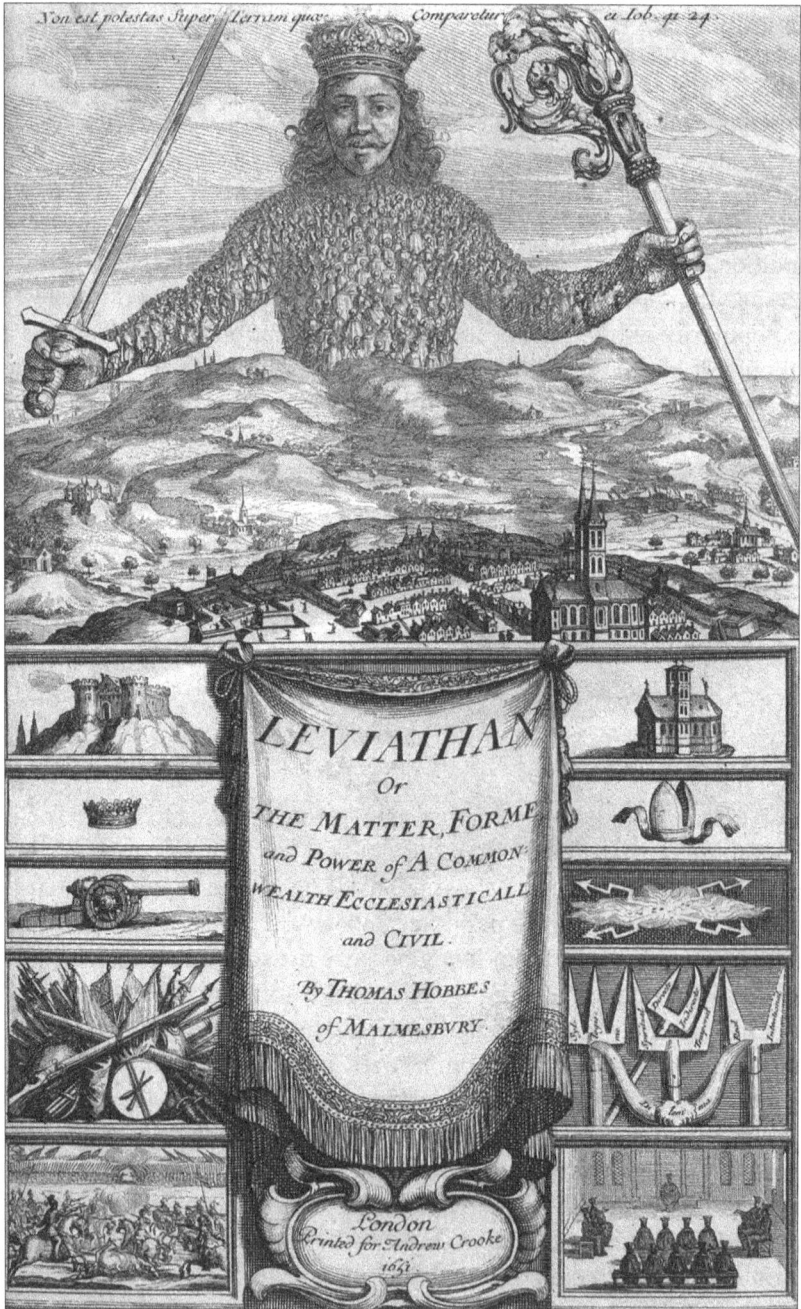

Figure 4.3. The frontispiece engraving to Thomas Hobbes's book *Leviathan.*

Meantime, unlike any ordinary individual, states do not remain exposed to the violent encroachments made upon their interests, since they do not have the same incapacities as private individuals. Even in the most trying situations, as Clausewitz had already noticed, there can be no doubt that a fight between any two individuals can end with a single blow; but a war between two countries may in practice extend beyond a certain battle. It was thus that, notwithstanding the deepened struggle betwixt the Soviet Union and the United States during the Cold War, the two superpowers looked on each other's sovereignty with mutual respect, indicating that a sort of society pervaded their connexion.

Still, however, in the history of the world, we find that kings and changing ministers have fed on the blood of people. So, the natural conclusion must be that, since war is a leading feature of sovereignty, this world, though extreme, takes into account the many wars which have occurred, and which are predicted to occur in the future, despite the existence of various features of international society in the field of international relations. As a result, it can be argued that since war is a normal feature of international relations, the extent and purpose of securing the advantages of a society of states cannot be carried into effect.[31]

The counterbalance to this order of things is found, speaking generally, in the very possibility of the reverses of war, since there begins to arise some chance of forming a society of states. Upon the whole, the original principles on which the theories aforesaid are founded seem equally applicable to world politics, in various degrees, at different times.

Retrospect

I am now to conclude my review of the formal interrogatories concerning the composition of the society of states. If we were to look back at the principal sentiments of theorists, from the alarms of realists to the letters of internationalists, we should see the train of societies which are to be found in the literature of most nations, with all their various histories, geographies and politics. It is sufficient to say, in conclusion, that Hedley Bull's idea of the "anarchical society" is agreeable to this summary proposition.

ENDNOTES

[1]   Andrew Linklater, "The English School Conception of International Society: Reflections on Western and Non-Western Perspectives," *Ritsumeikan Annual Review of International Studies* 9 (2010): 1–13.

[2]   Hedley Bull, *The Anarchical Society: A Study of Order in World Politics* (New York: Columbia University Press, 1977), 8.

[3]   Bull, *The Anarchical Society*, 9–10.

[4]   Bull, *The Anarchical Society*, 13.

[5]   David Armstrong, "The Evolution of International Society," in *The Globalization of World Politics: An Introduction to International Relations*, 5th ed., ed. John Baylis, Steve Smith, and Patricia Owens (Oxford: Oxford University Press, 2011), 37.

[6]   Armstrong, "The Evolution of International Society," 45.

[7]   Bull, *The Anarchical Society*, 24.

[8]   Bull, *The Anarchical Society*, 25.

[9]   Bull, *The Anarchical Society*, 25.

[10]   Bull, *The Anarchical Society*, 25.

[11]   Bull, *The Anarchical Society*, 25.

[12]   Thomas Hobbes, *Leviathan*, rev. student ed., ed. Richard Tuck (Cambridge: Cambridge University Press, 1996), 74.

[13]   Ian Clark, "International Society: (ii) Hedley Bull" (lecture, Aberystwyth University, Aberystwyth, Wales, October 29, 2013).

[14]   Bull, *The Anarchical Society*, 23.

[15]   Bull, *The Anarchical Society*, 24.

[16]   Bull, *The Anarchical Society*, 25–26.

[17]   Quoted in Farhang Rajaee, *Islamic Values and World View: Khomeyni on Man, the State and International Politics*, vol. 13 of *American Values Projected Abroad*, with a preface by Kenneth W. Thompson (Lanham, MD: University Press of America, 1983), 80.

[18]   David Armstrong, *Revolution and World Order: The Revolutionary State in International Society* (Oxford: Oxford University Press, 1993), 191.

[19]   Armstrong, *Revolution and World Order*, 192.

[20]   Armstrong, *Revolution and World Order*, 70.

[21]   Armstrong, "The Evolution of International Society," 36.

[22]   Bull, *The Anarchical Society*, 26.

[23]   Bull, *The Anarchical Society*, 27.

[24]   Bull, *The Anarchical Society*, 27.

[25]   Robert H. Jackson and Patricia Owens, "The Evolution in International Society," in *The Globalization of World Politics*, 3rd ed., ed. John Baylis and Steve Smith (Oxford: Oxford University Press, 2001), 58, quoted in Armstrong, "The Evolution of International Society," 46.

[26]   Armstrong, "The Evolution of International Society," 45.

[27]   Bull, *The Anarchical Society*, 38.

[28]   Bull, *The Anarchical Society*, 47.

[29]   Bull, *The Anarchical Society*, 48.

[30]   Bull, *The Anarchical Society*, 48.

[31]   Bull, *The Anarchical Society*, 46.

CHAPTER V

The European Parliament (EP) is under the daily and constant necessity of improving and strengthening the democratic legitimacy and the powers of its administration as an elected supranational institution in Europe. For this purpose, the EP signed the Treaty of Lisbon in December 2007. It is fair to add, however, that the EP is often regarded as insignificant, even after having brought about the widely felt and extensive reforms of the treaty. So stated, the following sections shall endeavor to state first the reasons for, and then the reply of, maintaining the EP.

Necessity of the European Parliament

Simon Hix, the famed political scientist, tells us in plain terms, that "the European Parliament successfully handles a massive policy agenda, and in most countries engages strongly with European citizens."[1] In fact, there are 150 to 200 pieces of legislation amended and scrutinized per year in addition to its oversight of "an annual budget of more than 120 billion Euros."[2] Besides monitoring the activities of the European Commission, the European Central Bank, and other agencies in the European Union (EU), the Parliament "also responds to numerous requests from citizens, interest groups, governments, political parties, journalists, trade associations, industries, trade unions, civil society organizations, and national politicians and civil servants" as an attempt to bring different "issues and viewpoints onto the EU's many different policy agendas."[3]

An example may be seen in the Society for Worldwide Interbank Financial Telecommunication (Swift) agreement signed by the EU and the United States of America, which induced the EU "to share information on all European citizens' financial transactions with the US Department of Homeland Security."[4] All the members of the EU appeared to accept the agreement. Yet, the agreement was subsequently thrown out "on the grounds that the deal committed the European Union to share data with the US authorities about EU citizens' transactions that the US government is not allowed to obtain about its own citizens under US law."[5] In other words, the rights of citizens were better safeguarded by the EP than by their national governments. Archick also asks whether "future US-EU information-sharing agreements may not be able to secure the necessary EP approval," after it was made known that the American intelligence services had spied on the EU's diplomatic offices.[6]

Figure 5.1. The European Parliamentary hemicycle in Brussels.

The new powers being vested in this assembly, therefore, have distinguished the EP in the eyes of the United States Congress. Indeed, as the president of the EP expressed it, the Treaty of Lisbon "gives a huge boost to the powers of the European Parliament. The rise in legislative powers for the European Parliament represents almost a doubling in power,"[7] so much so, that, "the EP and the Council of Ministers share legislative power and . . . the right to accept, amend, or reject proposed EU legislation."[8] Thus, for the first time, "the Lisbon Treaty strengthens the EP's role in the EU's legislative and budgeting processes, gives the EP the right to approve or reject international agreements, and bolsters the EP's decision-making authority on trade-related issues."[9] Archick, notwithstanding, asserts that "the EP's position in the annual budgetary process is now stronger than that of the Council, as the Council may never impose a budget against the will of the EP, but under some circumstances, the EP may impose a budget against the will of the Council."[10] If it means anything, it is remarkable also, that "EP committees rival those" within the Congress of the United States, "and surpass the role of committees in most national European legislatures."[11]

Moreover, the office of the Commission president is to be filled as the result of "a majority vote in the EP."[12] So circumstanced, it was understood that a "concrete and visible" connexion betwixt "voting in the elections and having a say in determining the future president of the European Commission" greatly improved the democratic legitimacy of the Parliament.[13] According to this agreement, it was natural to suppose that, directly or indirectly, "the party-political make-up of the next European Parliament will have a significant impact on the direction of the European Union . . . policy agenda."[14] It is further to be considered, that the EP is enabled to consent to the appointment of the foreign policy chief, or the vice-president of the Commission.

It is worthy of mention, that, in fact, "the French city of Strasbourg, which is close to the German border, was originally chosen as the seat of the EP to serve as a symbol of peace and reconciliation between the two countries."[15] The attempt, in short, to abolish the EP would weaken this symbol of peace between two historical enemies and revive the old disputes in Europe.

Views Against the European Parliament

Others, on the contrary, desire to see the EP terminated, and replaced by an indirectly elected assembly. Jack Straw, then foreign secretary of the United Kingdom, found the institution deficient in some points of democratic legitimacy.[16] It is evident, in surveying various elections, that turnout has fallen since the commencement of these events in 1979,[17] which, in comparison with the national elections, must have added much to the dismay of the trembling Europeanists. It may be supposed that the citizens of Europe had shown themselves almost persuaded of the political insignificance of these elections. It is manifest, indeed, that domestic affairs and the proceedings of domestic politicians predominate over the rest of the administration of the EP.[18] It has been said, the unhappy voters of each member state were equally awkward in their attempts to show their dissatisfaction with their governments. It seems also certain, that the different parties have contributed to the derangement of the fate of the European Community, merely because they have organized and financed election campaigns. So that candidates contrived to obtain votes as members, not of the European People's Party (EPP) or the Group of the Progressive Alliance of Socialists and Democrats (S&D), but of the French Socialist Party or the Christian Democratic Union of Germany.[19]

To add to these considerations, it is no wonder, given the multitude of their constituents, that a good many members of the European Parliament (MEPs) have experienced great difficulty in influencing the minds of their fellow citizens, with a view to increasing the popularity of the EP.[20] "The EU's legislative process," the Congressional Research Service reported to the United States Congress,

> is overly complex and often focused on highly technical issues, leading to a lack of public understanding about the role of the EP. Limited public awareness of the EP's activities, they maintain, is reflected in the consistently declining turnout in European Parliament elections. And while studies on voting behavior in the EP show that ideology holds greater influence than nationality (with MEPs voting with their party groups the vast majority of the time), many MEPs campaign for the European Parliament on national rather than European issues. Many voters also tend to view EP elections as national mid-term elections—an indication of voter opinion on the

performance of the national government—rather than as a vote on Europe-wide issues.[21]

This distinction is further exemplified in the unblushing demand of immense contributions in money, for example, to enable the movements of their politicians betwixt the cities of Brussels, Strasbourg, and Luxembourg at regular times. This is certainly true of procuring them the means of travel and accommodation. It seems to have been in general felt and admitted, that the EP has not done well in fulfilling its purpose of renewing the democratic forms of government. It is not fruitless to observe that, notwithstanding the extension of its powers, the EP has failed to achieve the same permanent importance as is granted to national parliaments.[22] On the whole, the degradation of the legitimacy of the EP shows neither support nor reserve, among the people, to avert the abolition of that legislative body.

The European Parliament's Significance Discussed

It would appear that the stipulations in favor of the EP are not strong enough to cause it to be respected. The result of Straw's observations has decided his opinion, "that the priorities the EU political elites continue to focus on are taking us away from core areas, such as tackling terrorism and international crime, where the public does in fact support close pan-European co-operation."[23] And when it is considered, that the EP cannot venture to propose its own laws, but to reject or amend the particulars of the proposals of the commissioners from the European Commission (EC), it may be in general observed that the powers of the EP are strained; while, in ordinary candor, it could be said to have represented the people, but unsuccessfully. The citizens of Europe, in short, looked rather to their national representatives than to the electoral bodies of Europe for the purpose of serving public interests of all kinds.

It was also whispered, that the EU became an object of more vague suspicion than formerly to the citizens in general; they thought the confidential relations between the EC and the European Council (EUCO) exhibited the failure of the EP to maintain the principles of democratic legitimacy and transparency, upon which the EU ought to rest.[24] It follows that, with the additional policy of the EC to consider citizens' initiatives, it may be doubtful whether the EP must remain an ornament of the city of

Strasbourg; for it must be acknowledged, a great number of citizens can induce the EC "to propose legislation in areas that fall within its competence."[25]

Lastly, persevering in the belief that the EP cannot be expected to improve its democratic legitimacy in spite of its newly given vigor, Lothar Bisky, who was then an MEP, has informed us, that "Parliament is actually not acting on its supposed new powers. Of course it has flexed its muscles to bring about some positive results, such as the rejection of the Swift agreement in February [2010]. But in the new vote on Swift [on July 8, 2010] it has certainly shown its unwillingness to defend European citizens."[26] This brings us back, then, to what we have already said: that, if the various MEPs fail to engage their constituents in a perpetual union, there shall be no hope for them; they will be unable to do any thing to maintain the authority they may possess.

Yet, before adopting the course that the discussion opened, the fact is, a great number of eligible persons are not intimately interested in the general deliberations of the state, or of Europe, and decline to vote in any election. The reader must, according to this general tendency, be aware, that the EP is not the only one of the kind to have had low electoral turnouts. We may remark also, that although the Treaty of Lisbon perhaps theoretically increased the powers with which the EP was supplied, it is a fallacy to suppose that such ground could be trod with ease. I leave it to journalists to inquire, whether the future destinies to which the EP might be summoned can be altered in proportion to the concoction of the new treaty.

Figure 5.2. Seat of the European Commission, at the Berlaymont building in Brussels.

General Conclusions

It is true, I cannot help but recall my resolution of neutrality between the desire to see the success of the EP and the sense that, its means of attaining the same object having been already overwhelmed, a long train of victory was utterly hopeless; and that, in consequence, the EP did not seem at length worthy of preservation. To sum up the whole, I took up my pen to present some knowledge of the direction and disposition of this institution, in the course of which it had received, as the result of the Treaty of Lisbon, increased powers, like a steam engine exposed to new combustibles; and to consider the extent of its importance to the general affairs of the whole European Union. I observed, that the democratic legitimacy of the EP's work and its own theatrical powers, in comparison to those of the other EU institutions and the national governments, might not be found equal to what their voters had probably expected. So captivating are the results of each election, like a puppet show, that we cannot help questioning the course of future elections.

This reserve, on the particulars of which we have dwelt the more especially, persuades us, for the present at least, of the political insignificance of the EP. To ensure such an outcome, however, the body of representatives should proceed to take measures to improve and strengthen the legitimacy of their official situations and their powers of action or legislation.

ENDNOTES

[1]   Simon Hix, "Why the European Parliament Should Not Be Abolished," *European Politics and Policy* (blog), March 5, 2012, https://blogs.lse.ac.uk/europpblog/2012/03/05/why-european-parliament-not-abolished/.

[2]   Hix, "Why the European Parliament Should Not Be Abolished."

[3]   Hix, "Why the European Parliament Should Not Be Abolished."

[4]   Hix, "Why the European Parliament Should Not Be Abolished."

[5]   Hix, "Why the European Parliament Should Not Be Abolished."

[6]   Kristin Archick, *The European Parliament*, CRS Report No. RS21998 (Washington, DC: Congressional Research Service, 2014), 14, https://sgp.fas.org/crs/row/RS21998.pdf.

[7]   Jerzy Buzek, "Statement by EP President Jerzy Buzek on the Lisbon Treaty," European Parliament, December 1, 2009, https://www.europarl.europa.eu/pdf/lisbon_treaty/statement_ep_president_EN.pdf.

[8]   Archick, *The European Parliament*, 2.

[9]   Archick, *The European Parliament*, 1.

[10]   Archick, *The European Parliament*, 4.

[11]   Archick, *The European Parliament*, 11.

[12]   Archick, *The European Parliament*, 5.

[13]   Archick, *The European Parliament*, 4.

[14]   Simon Hix, "Why the 2014 European Elections Matter: Ten Key Votes in the 2009–2013 European Parliament," *European Policy Analysis*, no. 15 (September 2013): 1, https://sieps.se/media/cmfjfa2b/why-the-2014-european-elections-matter_-ten-key-votes-in-the-2009-2013-european-parliament-2013_15epa.pdf.

[15]   Archick, *The European Parliament*, 13.

[16]   Patrick Wintour, "European Parliament Should Be Abolished, Says Jack Straw," *Guardian*, February 21, 2012, https://www.theguardian.com/world/2012/feb/21/european-parliament-abolish-jack-straw.

[17]   "Voter Turnout in the European Parliament Elections in the European Union (EU) from 1979 to 2024," Statista, released July 2024, https://www.statista.com/statistics/300427/eu-parlament-turnout-for-the-european-elections/.

[18]   Hix, "Why the European Parliament Should Not Be Abolished."

[19]   Michelle Cini and Nieves Pérez-Solórzano Borragán, eds., *European Union Politics*, 4th ed. (Oxford: Oxford University Press, 2013), 168.

[20]   Cini and Borragán, *European Union Politics*, 168.

[21]   Archick, *The European Parliament*, 13.

[22]   Archick, *The European Parliament*, 13.

[23]   Quoted in Wintour, "European Parliament Should Be Abolished, Says Jack Straw."

[24]   "Viewpoints: European Parliament Powers," BBC News, July 13, 2010, https://www.bbc.co.uk/news/10598594.

[25]   Koen Lenaerts, "The Principle of Democracy in the Case Law of the European Court of Justice," *International and Comparative Law Quarterly* 62, no. 2 (2013): 278, https://doi.org/10.1017/S0020589313000080.

[26]   BBC News, "Viewpoints: European Parliament Powers."

CHAPTER VI

A BATTLE BETWEEN NEOREALISTS, INSTITUTIONALISTS AND CONSTRUCTIVISTS REGARDING THE CONTINUATION OF POST–COLD WAR NATO OPERATIONS

I'll warrant that fellow from drowning,
were the ship no stronger than a nut-shell.

—*The Tempest*

After the Cold War, many were inclined to question the future of the North Atlantic Treaty Organization (NATO),[1] as the threat from the Union of Soviet Socialist Republics (USSR) was lost in a growling gargling sort of sound, the destroyer at once of NATO's *raison d'être*. It followed, however, from the sporty vivacity of those military conservators of NATO that scholars have attached to apparent marks of its evolution a degree of certainty, as far as it respects the alliance's prospects. Give me your patience, courteous readers, and I will illustrate the discrepancies of opinion with three theories sufficient to occupy the whole of this chapter. In the inside of the polemical case of International Relation (IR) theory is the usual assortment of neorealism, liberal institutionalism and social constructivism;[2] indeed, I will explain each more fully when I come to treat of recorded evidence in point of fact, and arguments in point of view, against and in favor of each projection and abutment, so that in these discoveries, the preservation of this multinational partiality is put in a tone meant to explain the concatenation of its context more distinctly. For my own part, I make a point not to express my internal conviction that one of the three theories into which the original model of IR is divided is more accurate than the prophecies of all the other IR theories. On the contrary, the incongruities of abstraction are so mingled with the interruption of historical narratives that I have endeavored to combine into a distinctive narrative, the well-furnished shelves and intricate passages from one set of IR theorists to the next, who might have influence upon the minds of all contending parties. It will be found that one theory's utmost pitch is inadequate to account for the affairs of this blue-covered round table along the Boulevard Léopold III.

There are four parts to this chapter, which should serve for my argument. The first part of this debate is simply the examination of the doctrine of the neorealists. In the succeeding parts (II and III), liberal institutionalism and social constructivism are weighed in the same methodological balance. I shall give a brief and true specimen of each succeeding theory, each quickly followed by some critical communications respecting the stoical endurance of the North Atlantic Alliance. So set forward, in the fourth section of the chapter, we then consider all these various lanes in seeking out a singular resolution to the polemical skirmishes between the three schools of neorealism, liberal institutionalism and social constructivism. Moreover, as a matter of direct evidence, it is necessary to place some circumstantial events, particularly concerning the conflict in Ukraine and the United States' foreign policy.

Hangman, or Neorealism

After the reign of the Soviets had been extinguished in the person of Mikhail Sergeyevich Gorbachev, the celebrated author of *Theory of International Politics*, Kenneth Waltz, believed that NATO had "outlived" its purpose and merits as the USSR's most inveterate and most formidable enemy.[3] To his extreme surprise, however, the alliance continued to press forward, like the clapper that thumps a bell's cracked sides, all the while advancing operations in the Republic of Kosovo (1998–1999), the Horn of Africa (2009–2016), the State of Libya (2011), and Afghanistan (2001–2021), etc. At any rate, some detail of alliance theory is necessary, in order to render intelligible the testimony of our pessimistic neorealists, who aver the calamitous circumstances in which countries find themselves.

Figure 6.1. Soviet General Secretary Gorbachev (left) and President Ronald Reagan (right) signing the Intermediate-Range Nuclear Forces (INF) Treaty in the White House.

"An alliance," according to Stephen Walt, "is a formal or informal commitment for security cooperation between two or more states. . . . The defining feature of any alliance is a commitment for mutual military support against some external actor(s) in some specified set of circumstances."[4] In this particular, Walt's current of thinking only illustrates the very important and general proposition, concerning the dismantling of the old star, and the disuse of the compass. For, ever since 1991, it has seemed improbable that the Western Bloc should again expect to suffer a disorder of violent resistance, especially since, as matters stood, they conceived they need not contend with the assaults of the wily enemy of capitalism. In his "Why Alliances Endure or Collapse?" (1997) Walt records the three principal reasons for the termination of alliances: a changing view of the gnashing teeth of danger, the precariousness of credibility, and domestic politics. In this enumeration neorealists could have expected NATO's suddenly breaking asunder. In the first place, the US had no reason to stay in NATO, because the vehement threat of communism was past and gone, and because the US had gained a hegemonic footling in the world, the possession of some economic prowess, the reputation of more, and a growing disposition to increase its highly technical slaughter-weapons, such as are illustrated by nuclear weapons, which dart at her enemies a bald eagle glance that makes the limbs tremble, and the knee bend. Besides, they could then hope to cut off the supply of money to the collective body. The outcome, therefore, could be fairly imputed to no other motive than self-defense.

But, notwithstanding these neorealist prejudices, the rest of the gang jumped on the transatlantic bandwagon, out of regard for their own profit or security.[5] Certainly, as Walt observes, hegemonic leadership may be alleged as a reason for the endurance of some of our alliances.[6] There is also an ambitious rival, namely, in the Far East, whose progressively increasing (silky) purses and (shining) armories loom rather as an aspirant threat, with all its necessary consequences to the West. They (NATO members) need each other's assistance, like a company crossing a mountainous xiangyun (auspicious cloud), and are compelled to clasp together, lest the collected breath of China's dragon should become too powerful for any who are not thus canvassed or bolstered up.[7] Walt has stated in the article before mentioned, that NATO provides "an impediment to regional competition and a hedge against a rising and increasingly assertive China."[8]

But being interrogated, the neorealist approach to inter-national relations may not be highly useful in accounting for the cold tone of light acquiescence with which Canada and the US speak together, despite the occasional quiver of a shifting balance of power in their own eyes. In other respects, the first Secretary General of NATO, Hastings Ismay, after he had retired, pronounced the vindictive purpose of the body: "to keep the Russians out, the Americans in, and the Germans down,"[9] which implies that the tirade against the USSR, as intimated in the pourtraictures of the red guards, given unto the public in general, was not its sole purpose. To be sure, the assembly, if we may presume still to inquire into the transactions of its member states, already evinces tokens of the opposite consequences from what the neorealists had prophesied. With this easy sweep of outline, which at once indicates various causes, we are under the necessity of entertaining other theories.

The Fairy Tale of Liberal Institutionalism?

In attempting to introduce liberal institutionalism, the author felt himself bound to quote a few words in order to abridge the period of deliberation. On this subject, Walt proceeds to say, that NATO has endured in consequence of "its long duration, diverse capabilities and demonstrated capacity to amend doctrines and organizational forms in response to external developments."[10] And as for Robert B. McCalla, NATO continued its course through all the billows of institutional mechanism, which suffered it to adapt to the succession of changing security circumstances,[11] a course that contrasts "with the traditional conception of an alliance as a compact between sovereign states."[12] In fact, Walt thought that NATO's "highly institutionalized, . . . elaborate decision-making procedures and . . . extensive supporting bureaucracy" were unlike "the Axis alliance of 1939–45 or most inter-Arab alliances, which were limited partnerships in which each member acted relatively independently."[13] In short, like a cultivated field, "death will take substantially longer in an alliance with a well-developed organizational entity attached to it."[14]

But, upon the whole, as to the criticism which it received, Barany and Rauchhaus inform us, that notwithstanding the various advantages—namely, those of highly institutionalized joint decision-making procedures, with the simplicity of its well-defined rules, meant to facilitate the involvement of a unified military command structure—these advantages could only delay the ultimate discontinuation of NATO.[15] It is very possible that a wholesale transformation, internally or externally, might compel NATO to divide, in the same justifiable light in which neorealists themselves consider it. Truly, it may well be supposed that "NATO as an organization will have at times interests that are different than those of its members, much like corporate officials can sometimes have different interests from shareholders."[16] If so, it cannot "be surprising to see clashes between NATO officials and member state officials over the continued need for the alliance."[17] Still, however, there is another train of ideas, called social constructivism, which I think might be creditably considered, as the source of a different interpretation.

Social Constructivism's Cairn

It often happens that being part of a political community, individual actors may "no longer think of themselves as wholly separable units."[18] It is worth mentioning, the North Atlantic Treaty dictates that the parties to the treaty "are determined to safeguard the freedom, common heritage and civilization of their peoples, founded on the principles of democracy, individual liberty and the rule of law."[19] That is to say, gentle reader, that social constructivists believe NATO in the meantime "helped create a transatlantic security community with shared values" and norms.[20] It is scarcely necessary to say, distinctly, that social constructivists see the international arena as "an anarchy of friends," but not as the neorealist "anarchy of enemies."[21] In one sense, indeed, it seems as if "norms are what make institutions work."[22] An argument clearly supplementing liberal institutionalism, but at the same time revealing the latter theory's trouble in explaining NATO's new existence. To borrow from Vincent Pouliot, who describes the concept of security community: it need not be "idyllic instances of international relations," or "the absence of conflicts among its members, but instead *the peaceful resolution* of such conflicts" (italics in the original).[23] Pouliot continues, "power is what makes the social construction of reality possible," and it is "part of the process by which norms and other sociopolitical realities are constituted."[24]

But anyhow, I would like to take an early opportunity to propose that Samuel Huntington's notion of the "clash of civilizations" may easily lead astray skillful train of social constructivist suggestions.[25] Huntington's narrative throws light on the Eastern end of the era of ideological conflict, with the final cry of the Soviet Union, and shows another offspring of this miserable history, no less powerful: the cultural conflict betwixt the seven or so fretful and supercilious civilizations (named Western, Orthodox, Islamic, Hindu, African, Latin American, Sinic, and Japanese traditions). From this difference of cultural identity betwixt them, it happens that, excepting two or more "torn" countries, the many cases of unity appear necessary for NATO's (Western) comfort.

Having the general sentiments of social constructivism thus confirmed, the said theory may be instantly attacked upon certain points of controversy. Walt remarks, "National leaders are prone to describe their allies in overly flattering terms, and to overstate the level of compatibility and identification between them."[26] He adds, that "a sense of common identity may slow the process of dissolution for quite some time, but the level of solidarity and mutual identification is not strong enough to prevent states from pursuing an independent course once their interests begin to conflict."[27] And if there appears a fair prospect of disagreement and disunion concerning the management of foreign and domestic policy, those decision makers would probably attend to the domestic concerns of their fellow citizens, as they "owe their careers to how well they satisfy their own electorates."[28] It is not, perhaps, the most striking instance of the impelling motive by which the peace of the national delegations at Brussels is liable to be shaken, but the Bosnian War in Bosnia and Herzegovina showed, "unity cannot be taken for granted."[29] Furthermore, the "Atlantic Community," which is perhaps much exaggerated, does not admit the tolerance of those member states (Portuguese Republic, Hellenic Republic, Republic of Türkiye, as some people have said) known to have had a share in undemocratic practices. Similarly, Webber, Sperling and Smith advance in a few words: "The post-9/11 agenda of Afghanistan, Iraq, terrorism and WMD [weapon of mass destruction], however, has meant NATO has been diverted into areas of concern where its collective identity is not at stake."[30]

Figure 6.2. President Harry S. Truman (seated) signs a proclamation declaring into effect the 12-nation North Atlantic Pact.

Author's Analysis

Thus far, I have reviewed the three theories in IR scholarship—neorealism, liberal institutionalism and social constructivism—and soon found that the tinge of pedantry, which naturally flows from reflection, renders them less refined when they are left alone. After all, Barany and Rauchhaus believe "none of the three theories perform well in isolation at predicting or explaining NATO's adaptation to the post–Cold War environment"; whereas, "when combined, these IR theories can offer a coherent explanation for the alliance's enlargement and the development of out-of-area operations."[31] I, therefore, form a singular resolution for the purpose of abridging the steep and slippery ascent and descent on which these theories are still visible, the execution of which forms the subject of this section. I will not stop until I have occupied a noisy cable car intended for the accommodation of our three "-ism" guides.

Indeed, as we eye the approach of our intersectional coach, while raking through the whole train of learned disquisitions on the nature of NATO's continuation, it may be proper to apprise the neorealist reader that the forcible annexation of Crimea by the Russian Federation in February and March of 2014 gave NATO an opportunity for farther consolidation in the strong fervency of its security community and international institutionalism, whereby it could contrive to keep itself alive. As *The Economist* has noticed, NATO's objection to military aggression suggested "that Article 5 remained the unshakable pillar of the alliance."[32] There is ground to think, that the march of Britain's troops (a thousand military personnel and one hundred armored vehicles) to Poland nourished a parade of precaution.[33] On perusing the chronicles of the various aerial patrols that the Russians had established in different parts of the Caribbean and the Gulf of Mexico, it is thought, the eventful operations recalled the whole proceedings of the Cuban Missile Crisis;[34] although it seemed to the president himself, Barack Hussein Obama II, that the People's Republic of China (PRC) was a greater threat to the US than Russia, uniformly acknowledging the diverging interests of the US and its transatlantic counterparts in NATO; totally regardless of the usual rhetorical hook of ring leaders.[35]

Chomsky, more calm and considerate, critically strikes at the root of the matter, by a gentle recapitulation of the enterprise of NATO as an instrument of US foreign policy.[36] In fact, since the year 1949, when the Washington Treaty was signed, the US has made a permanent impression of favor necessary to secure the ascendancy of its own progress and event. Thus far, therefore, the fate of NATO has more or less depended upon agendas peculiar to the US, more than it has on other NATO member states. In this comprehensive sense, the US, in order to raise some strength to reinforce its power in the wilderness of the world, shouldered the expansion of NATO as a movable anvil disposed against the newly expanding Western frontier provinces along the various lands which led to the heart of old Mother Russia where hammermen and sicklemen worked the mighty machine and reaped their jovial harvest; for probably there was no other alternative which would have cost them little; and hence it happens that this condition became the means of maintaining this military superstructure at the seat of collective defense. The author can only add to this narrative that if the US were to separate itself from the communion of the established military and unload its inestimable burden-sharing obligations, the poorer partakers of the pact, strongly moved by the economic hardships of the financial crisis, may not take an enthusiastic view of paying the next term's stipend. And then, if it may seem in some degree severe, it is full time to await the death of NATO. The United States' contribution, which at one point came nearly to seventy per cent, serves as an illustration of its importance.[37]

To the explanation of the neorealist hypothesis, the institutionalist and social constructivist answer, that though the sight of an enemy may sometimes attract and hold different parties together, the past history of eventful strivings and escapes, structural shifts, and seizures exercises considerable influence over future prospects. To cut the matter short, neorealism does not at all times willingly submit to the presence of the newly formed community, in the center of which we hear the penetrating motto, *animus in consulendo liber* (a mind unfettered in deliberation). At the same time, we must not forget the yoke of domestic factors, from the dross of imprudent and unjustifiable elite interests and ideological hegemony, etc., that betoken a slow step or two to the round table to keep the peace of the Republic of Bosnia and Herzegovina, assuming the tenet, that the crisis did not relate to their domestic political sentiments.[38]

Tolling to Conclusion

In this laconic epistle, so narrow was the chasm out of which we ascended, that, unless the eye and the imagination of the reader followed first one theory then another, till they caught hold of the discourse beyond each factious description, NATO, it may readily be conceived, is a complex, multifaceted coalition, embroidered to match the intricate nexus of our international politics, which would seem to commission an amalgamated composition of the three theories illustrated by substantial proofs, and which I have endeavored honestly to obtain. It is plain that, amid its incoherence, a hybrid of theories of different habits of scholarship cannot at all times alike be supposed to possess the summative key necessary to reconcile the speculative principles with future consequences. I hope I have maintained my testimony on the causes and effects of NATO's journey, whereof run the deep waters of the Atlantic Ocean.

ENDNOTES

1   NATO member countries include Albania, Belgium, Bulgaria, Canada, Croatia, Czechia, Denmark, Estonia, Finland, France, Germany, Greece, Hungary, Iceland, Italy, Latvia, Lithuania, Luxembourg, Montenegro, Netherlands, North Macedonia, Norway, Poland, Portugal, Romania, Slovakia, Slovenia, Spain, Sweden, Türkiye, United Kingdom, United States.

2   Zoltan Barany and Robert Rauchhaus, "Explaining NATO's Resilience: Is International Relations Theory Useful?," *Contemporary Security Policy* 32, no. 2 (2011): 286–307, https://doi.org/10.1080/13523260.2011.590355.

3   Kenneth N. Waltz, "Structural Realism After the Cold War," *International Security* 25, no. 1 (Summer 2000): 5–41, https://www.jstor.org/stable/2626772.

4   Stephen M. Walt, "Why Alliances Endure or Collapse," *Survival* 39, no. 1 (1997): 157, https://doi.org/10.1080/00396339708442901.

5   Mark Webber, James Sperling, and Martin A. Smith, *NATO's Post-Cold War Trajectory: Decline or Regeneration?* (Basingstoke, UK: Palgrave Macmillan, 2012), 34.

6   Walt, "Why Alliances Endure or Collapse," 156–179.

7   Michael Barr, *Who's Afraid of China? The Challenge of Chinese Soft Power* (London: Zed Books, 2011).

8   Walt, "Why Alliances Endure or Collapse," 171.

9   Quoted in Victor Davis Hanson, "Lord Ismay, NATO, and the Old-New World Order," *National Review*, July 5, 2017, https://www.nationalreview.com/2017/07/nato-russians-out-americans-germans-down-updated-reversed/.

10   Walt, "Why Alliances Endure or Collapse," 167.

11   Robert B. McCalla, "NATO's Persistence After the Cold War," *International Organization* 50, no. 3 (Summer 1996): 445–475, https://www.jstor.org/stable/2704032.

12   Walt, "Why Alliances Endure or Collapse," 168.

13   Walt, "Why Alliances Endure or Collapse," 157.

14   McCalla, "NATO's Persistence After the Cold War," 470.

15   Barany and Rauchhaus, "Explaining NATO's Resilience," 286–307.

16   McCalla, "NATO's Persistence After the Cold War," 456.

17   McCalla, "NATO's Persistence After the Cold War," 457.

18   Walt, "Why Alliances Endure or Collapse," 168.

19   North Atlantic Treaty, April 4, 1949, https://www.nato.int/cps/en/natohq/official_texts_17120.htm.

[20]   Barany and Rauchhaus, "Explaining NATO's Resilience," 292.

[21]   Martin Griffiths, Terry O'Callaghan, and Steven C. Roach, *International Relations: The Key Concepts*, 2nd ed. (Abingdon, UK: Routledge, 2008), 8.

[22]   Webber, Sperling, and Smith, *NATO's Post-Cold War Trajectory*, 44.

[23]   Vincent Pouliot, "The Alive and Well Transatlantic Security Community: A Theoretical Reply to Michael Cox," *European Journal of International Relations* 12, no. 1 (2006): 120, https://doi.org/10.1177/1354066106061332.

[24]   Pouliot, "The Alive and Well Transatlantic Security Community," 119–127.

[25]   Samuel P. Huntington, "The Clash of Civilizations?," *Foreign Affairs* 72, no. 3 (Summer 1993): 22–49, https://doi.org/10.2307/20045621.

[26]   Walt, "Why Alliances Endure or Collapse," 169.

[27]   Walt, "Why Alliances Endure or Collapse," 170.

[28]   Walt, "Why Alliances Endure or Collapse," 169.

[29]   Walt, "Why Alliances Endure or Collapse," 170.

[30]   Webber, Sperling, and Smith, *NATO's Post-Cold War Trajectory*, 43.

[31]   Barany and Rauchhaus, "Explaining NATO's Resilience," 287.

[32]   "NATO Flexes Its Muscle Memory," *The Economist*, August 30, 2014, https://www.economist.com/international/2014/08/30/nato-flexes-its-muscle-memory.

[33]   "British Army in NATO Black Eagle Exercise," BBC News, November 21, 2014, https://www.bbc.co.uk/news/uk-30142764.

[34]   Jonathan Masters, "The North Atlantic Treaty Organization (NATO)," Council on Foreign Relations, August 5, 2014, https://web.archive.org/web/20141223105816/http://www.cfr.org/nato/north-atlantic-treaty-organization-nato/p28287; "Russian Planes to Patrol in Caribbean, Gulf of Mexico," BBC News, November 12, 2014, https://www.bbc.co.uk/news/world-europe-30028371.

[35]   Masters, "The North Atlantic Treaty Organization (NATO)."

[36]   Noam Chomsky, "The Credibility of NATO: Noam Chomsky Interviewed by Mary Lou Finlay," by Mary Lou Finlay, *As It Happens*, April 16, 1999, https://chomsky.info/19990416/.

[37]   Masters, "The North Atlantic Treaty Organization (NATO)."

[38]   Walt, "Why Alliances Endure or Collapse," 161–163.

CHAPTER VII

ON THE ROLE OF ISLAM IN MAKING FOREIGN POLICY:
THE CLASH OF CIVILIZATIONS

We heard the Techir—so these Arabs call
Their shout of onset, when, with loud acclaim,
They challenge Heaven to give them victory.

—Sir Walter Scott, *The Talisman*

The burning sun of Valencia had not yet set, when a soldier of the Prophet, who had joined the host of the Muslims in Spain, galloped along the rocky cliffs that lie in the vicinity of the Mediterranean, to lay the command upon poets, music makers, doctors and scientists, in the name of "the One God, the True God—Allah," to rule Spain, then Europe, then the whole world. The fiery and overbearing character of Ben Yusuf constituted the principal antagonist of the charming film *El Cid*, starring Charlton Heston as the Christian knight Don Rodrigo Díaz de Vivar. Some say this was but a clash of religions betwixt the Christian and Saracen camps; some that its splendor consisted rather more in that brilliancy of complexion which savored of the miraculous—at least, since the Çid was and promised to forward an especial alliance with the Spanish Muslims.

Still, it must be allowed that Samuel P. Huntington could not help but declaring that he prophesied the horrors of war in the midst of the clash of civilizations—not least since the days of the Cold War. An inexorable fate, perhaps, that became the subject of his most controversial book, *The Clash of Civilizations and the Remaking of World Order*, in which he at length pitched the importance of the motives of religion that usually flow, by looks, gestures, or signs, from the tabernacle of each civilization. Huntington led the way accordingly toward visions of conquest and of glory, as occasioned by the power of religion to make foreign policy. The reader may be curious to know if Huntington's thesis is acceptable in the sight of truth. It is indeed our purpose in placing Islam in front of our sable and glittering eyes, to see how an outline of the clash might be traced on its clanging broadsword and shield.

Figure 7.1. Christian and Muslim playing chess, painted in the Middle Ages.

Hence, I will first unclasp the book already mentioned and I will survey the power of religious pursuits to frame foreign policy, that is according to the opinion expressed by Huntington regarding the clash of civilizations. In the second section, I cast a glance of examination on criticisms very unfavorable to Huntington and his message. I furnish forth specimens of Islamic countries which might illustrate the various points of the hypothesis in each section.

Comparatively, I will venture into the camp of the Islamic Republic of Iran. Presently afterwards, I will myself hold communication with other critical confessors to discuss the general role of religions in making foreign policy, in order to get as much knowledge as possible of the canons which denounce the infamous plot in which Huntington was engaged. I will conclude that the assured tokens which the American professor had exhibited were not entirely sufficient to explain the state of international politics.

Let the Trumpets Sound

Now, speaking conjecturally, Carolyn M. Warner and Stephen G. Walker, in their article, "Thinking About the Role of Religion in Foreign Policy: A Framework for Analysis," argue corresponding rhymes betwixt the hypochondriacal effusions of the realist school of international relations and Professor Huntington's clash of civilizations.[1] Apparently, the parallel is to be seen in the values of nations, which may proceed to the inner tabernacle of another, and from thence are readier to avoid the crying of war-cries to counteract each other. In plain language, those very countries that share in the same religious practices and principles are unlikely to find the daggers, of their cultural and religious neighbors, glancing at their very throats.[2] Literally, if fully encountered, the clash of civilizations foresees that the large-scale conflicts of futurity will be the consequence of the marked difference among civilizations, instead of the former ideological strife between capitalism and communism.[3] Accordingly, Huntington assures the sounding of gathering-notes upon trumpets, pipes, clarions, drums, tabors, bugles, bagpipes, and cymbals, by which the different troops are gathered to their African, Latin American, Slavic-Orthodox, Hindu, Islamic, Confucian, and Western civilizations' banners.[4]

Verily, the acknowledged supporters of the clash of civilizations have offered pregnant examples: the United States' invasions of the Islamic Emirate of Afghanistan and the Republic of Iraq, the direct and unvarnished attacks on September 11, 2001, committed by al-Qaeda, or, as if to show itself more distinctly, the rise of Islamist parties around the time of the First Arab Spring.[5] Or, more familiarly, the esquires of Huntington's distinct idea allude to the fanning of discord between the United States of America and the People's Republic of China, which contend themselves with pursuing the contest in soft power, culturally, politically, economically, educationally, technologically, diplomatically, and socially.[6] Therefore, we have been informed that the hand of Huntington has been heavy upon the various scenes of the Oriental night, in foreign policy, if a layman may say so much.

The Terror of Criticism's Fangs

But yet, methinks, all yonder clash and clang cannot be sufficient to subdue other considerations; for, at the same instant, the discord between political scientists is fanned by the dauntless determination of one of the most enlightened philosophers of the Jewish world, Professor Noam Chomsky (along by the side of Norman Gary Finkelstein, Jeffrey David Sachs, Howard Zinn). Yea, it has been abundant as the fountain of reason which springs up from beneath the shade of a true descendant of Israel, who, galloping at full career, has described the manners and vices of his nation, whom, after all, no remonstrance has yet induced to challenge the Kingdom of Saudi Arabia or Republic of Indonesia to mortal combat.[7] Let me be pardoned if I inquire the real reason behind the mystery attendant on this matter. For Chomsky, and other guards of the words of truth, it appears that there are some scenes of contention in which we are probably to look for a "clash of interests,"[8] rather than a clash of cultures or, as our "Mad Dog" says,[9] civilizations. The clash of interests, in this climate, converts the interests of each different country into something almost as unstable as economic and political motives, hidden under an appearance of democracy! Democracy! The democracy of the Silicon Valley! The arsenal of surveillance capitalism! I speak of that country but as all people speak who have seen it in the field of battle, whose sole object of its expedition in the Middle East has been to fulfil Netanyahu's strategic demands, and, by the power of violent exertion, to torment the Jews, Christians and Muslims of the Holy Land. Meantime, events have taken place quite contrary to the suppositions which Huntington had entertained. See you not that, although the Republic of Indonesia contains the largest number of Mohammedans than any other nation, there is no real cause for weal and woe, arising from religious warfare with the Western Christians. At vespers (or *Maghrib* prayers), I might again, with your leave, inquire whether the clash of the civilizations remains with the shadow or the substance of all foreign policy and of courtly art?

The Productions of a Persian Simurgh's Dream

Yet, hold! let me first examine the theocracy of the Islamic Republic of Iran as an example to those who account themselves the followers of Huntington's crusade. When the mainstream media announced the relationship between the United States and Iran, hitherto generally known, where the crusaders lay expecting swords thirsting for the blood of the servants of the Lord, yet it seems that the issue was written in the book of realist international relations theory, which seems to administer labor for the interest of the elite class of their encampment.[10] Surely, if the United States is so incensed at the progress of the land of poets and mystics' nuclear enterprise, they have certainly some reason to fear that it would blemish their alliances and might set an example to their regional neighbors who would be encouraged to reject the counsel of that imperial superpower, for the defense of their own independence;[11] and it oftentimes happens that, notwithstanding their own jealous vigilance, on account of their unholy enterprise, they have received it from their corporate masters. Interestingly enough, the Racket—that modern Leviathan of war and profit—understands not, or heeds not, the prohibition against nuclear weapons dictated by the Supreme Leader, at the 16th Summit of the Non-Aligned Movement in Tehran, when he said, "The Islamic Republic of Iran considers the use of nuclear, chemical and similar weapons as a great and unforgivable sin," with an emphasis on the motto of his nation: "Nuclear energy for all and nuclear weapons for none."[12]

Figure 7.2. Location: Nagorno-Karabakh near the border of the Islamic Republic of Iran.

Yet further, the close conflict over Nagorno-Karabakh in which the Shia Muslim Azeris of the Republic of Azerbaijan and Armenian Apostolic Christians of the Republic of Armenia have long been engaged, has not inspired Islamist Iran to come, in the same Shiite's garb, to the former's assistance.[13] "Iran," said the expounder of *The Limits of Culture: Islam and Foreign Policy*, Brenda Shaffer, "prefers Baku to be embroiled in a conflict and unable to serve as a source of attraction for the Azerbaijanis in Iran," who are acknowledged to be the largest ethnic minority in the country.[14] Neither has its foreign policy prioritized Islamic solidarity, founded upon Islamic principles, in the Tajikistani Civil War (1992–1997), the First Chechen War (1994–1996), the Second Chechen War (1999–2009), notwithstanding its usual decided rhetoric.[15] Indeed, despite Mahmoud Ahmadinejad's stern antagonism against the United States during his presidential incumbency (2005–2013), the two countries did not enter into war with each other. As it was, Hassan Rouhani (2013–2021) pursued a "centrist-pragmatic agenda,"[16] which was necessary to carry on the diplomatic negotiations with the P5+1 (China, France, Russia, the United Kingdom, and the United States; plus Germany) about the nuclear program of the Islamic Republic. All these considerations authorize caution concerning the conflict of civilizations, as Huntington had perceived by the shadowy wall of the secular caverns of the Hollow Earth! and remind us how necessary it is that we should become sensible and apprehensive of the power of the philosophy of history fostered by the learned and ingenious mind of that matchless champion of the words of truth, called Oswald Arnold Gottfried Spengler (1880–1936), who, as he was aware, regained the historical path of the sun, moon, and stars, so that he must needs be called the Diamond of the Desert, which promised the refreshment of living water.

Figure 7.3. Oswald Spengler, German polymath and author of *The Decline of the West* (1918 and 1922).

To sum the whole, Huntington's Central Intelligence Agency–sponsored commission to draw the curtain of futurity inclined me to presume somewhat upon the pillars which supported his high mission to the sinful progenitures of the prophet Musa's twelve spies. It has been a main object of Iran's foreign policy to intercede in favor of its national interests; but in no direction can we see traces of religious scruples, thanks to the blessings of the prophets, who, for Shiites, consist of Jesus (Īsā ibn Maryam), John the Baptist (Yaḥyā ibn Zakariyā), Abraham (Ibrahim), Moses (Mūsā ibn ʿImrān), etc.[17] In fact, the Koranic concept of an "ummah," uniting *Müslümans* of all the various nations assembled, according to their cultural, traditional, and religious resemblance, has borne not the weight even of a grain of sand in its progress and event, which could restore the banner of the Crescent upon conquered fields of battle betwixt terrified challengers and defenders.[18] Yet it is evident that the ummah is only "a matter of moral and emotional solidarity, nothing more."[19] Having found Huntington's horse peculiarly unfit for journeying around the limb of the tree Methuselah, I will presently give my attention to various habits of society, or states of politics and opinions entertained therewithal, that might affect foreign policy making in Muslimdom.

A Grain of Dust

Carolyn M. Warner and Stephen G. Walker, to whom the real import of institutions (endowed with constitutions and laws), geopolitical circumstances or position, the pressure of interest groups or public opinion, and cultural heritage (the distinctions of domestic religion, identity, tradition) upon the foreign policy of those nations that look towards the holy city of Makkah al-Mukarramah—is well known, have pointed out how they might influence "agents"—leaders and chiefs of crusades or jihads (which concepts, above all, referred to the warlike pilgrimage to struggle against sinful desires that war against one's own soul), who come to such decisions.[20] This examination, on looking more closely, seems consistent with the two levels of analysis in which, according to what J. David Singer has learned, the international system and the national state are placed.[21] To this analytic equipment was added, as Valerie M. Hudson, Christopher S. Vore licensed, like Warner and Walker, not without evident reluctance, the supplementary level of the bureaucratic engine.[22]

Still further to dispel the heavy grasp of the Albert J. Weatherhead III University Professor, and a loose network of his best-mounted cavaliers, from our shoulders, there are some instances also in which the executioners of the war on terror, and the mainstream media or television-scape of the West, are seen to treat Islam as more a militant religion than as a religion guided by the five pillars, while at the same time continuing the export of a pure and simple globalized democracy. In plain language, then, Bill Maher added a commentary ("the only religion that acts like the mafia" and which would "fucking kill you if you say the wrong thing, draw the wrong picture or write the wrong book"), which provoked much room for the ebullition of heated passions, enacted upon a talk show stage.[23] So that, contrary to Mohammed Arkoun's expectation, where the banners of fundamentalist groups like Al-Qaeda or Daesh stand, one assumes to have noticed the presence of the emblem of Islam, but not the reality, of tolerance and a unifying force in many respects.[24] Whatever may be the prejudices of every people against their neighbors, I undertake not to deny that some of these are excited by the cynical hatred and contempt of all besides. Meanwhile social engineering, so successfully handled by the dark mass of mainstream media, gradually and imperceptibly gives way to the gate of the labyrinth of lies and deceptions that create an internal chain of artificial shade by which their intuitive feelings, both mental and natural, are disguised and obscured. Their predilective adulation for the clash of civilizations, in the meantime, augments their confusion by insisting, as if to manufacture consent, that there is an ideological calling resting upon distinctions among religions.[25]

Conclusion to Chapter

In a word, I have loosened the bonds which have held Huntington's bunch of thoughts on civilizatory clashes; you saw the structural cord which was cut into four sectional pieces. I accordingly introduced the thesis composed by that controversial figure of political science. After this exordium, I began a critique of the theory, intermixed with examples. Thus conjured, I called forth, in reference to Iran's foreign policy gesticulations, some general expostulations concerning Huntingtonianism; and, finally, I questioned the effect of the blessed religion of which each civilization hath partaken. The clash of civilizations, in short, assures that the Islamic civilization, like the imprisoned tiger that would burst from the iron barriers of its cage, will thrust its long saber into a quarrel with an infidel whom it cannot bind in an alliance. Albeit, closer inspection discerned in our thoughts that case which was altogether so uncommon, when, the reader must remember, singular contrasts to the purpose of waging a war step from the shadow into the moonlight, for more than one thousand and one nights. Come, we must needs continue our conference at the Saracen's Head Inn, Gallowgate, Glasgow, to inquire distinctly into the nature and extent of the connection betwixt religion and culture as Dr. Samuel at least suggested!

ENDNOTES

[1]   Carolyn M. Warner and Stephen G. Walker, "Thinking About the Role of Religion in Foreign Policy: A Framework for Analysis," *Foreign Policy Analysis* 7, no. 1 (January 2011): 113–135, https://doi.org/10.1111/j.1743-8594.2010.00125.x.

[2]   Warner and Walker, "Thinking About the Role of Religion in Foreign Policy."

[3]   Samuel P. Huntington, "The Clash of Civilizations?," *Foreign Affairs* 72, no. 3 (Summer 1993): 22–49, https://doi.org/10.2307/20045621.

[4]   Huntington, "The Clash of Civilizations?," 22–49.

[5]   Khaled Diab, "The Invasion of Iraq and the Clash Within Civilizations," HuffPost, May 21, 2013, https://www.huffpost.com/entry/clash-of-civilizations-iraq_b_2922448.

[6]   Michael Barr, *Who's Afraid of China? The Challenge of Chinese Soft Power* (London: Zed Books, 2011).

[7]   Noam Chomsky, "Militarism, Democracy and People's Right to Information" (lecture, Delhi School of Economics, New Delhi, India, November 5, 2001), https://www.india-seminar.com/2002/509/509%20noam%20chomsky.htm.

[8]   Chomsky, "Militarism, Democracy and People's Right to Information"; Diab, "The Invasion of Iraq and the Clash Within Civilizations."

[9]   Andrew J. Gawthorpe, " 'Mad Dog?' Samuel Huntington and the Vietnam War," *Journal of Strategic Studies* 41, no. 1–2 (2018): 301–325, https://doi.org/10.1080/01402390.2016.1265510.

[10]   Noam Chomsky, "The Iranian Threat," Chomsky.info, July 2, 2010, https://chomsky.info/20100702/.

[11]   Chomsky, "The Iranian Threat."

[12]   Quoted in Seyed Hossein Mousavian, "Five Options for Iran's New President," *Cairo Review of Global Affairs*, no. 10 (Summer 2013): 68–79, https://crescent.icit-digital.org/articles/nuclear-energy-for-all-and-nuclear-weapons-for-none-the-rahbar.

[13]   Svante E. Cornell, "Religion as a Factor in Caucasian Conflicts," *Civil Wars* 1, no. 3 (Autumn 1998): 46–64, https://www.silkroadstudies.org/resources/pdf/publications/1-religionfactor.pdf; Brenda Shaffer, "The Islamic Republic of Iran: Is It Really?," in *The Limits of Culture: Islam and Foreign Policy*, ed. Brenda Shaffer (Cambridge, MA: MIT Press, 2006), 219-239.

[14]   Shaffer, "The Islamic Republic of Iran," 229.

[15]   Shaffer, "The Islamic Republic of Iran," 219–239.

[16]   Mahmood Monshipouri and Manochehr Dorraj, "Iran's Foreign Policy: A Shifting Strategic Landscape," *Middle East Policy* 20, no. 4 (Winter 2013): 133, https://doi.org/10.1111/mepo.12052.

[17]   Mohammad Javad Zarif, "What Iran Really Wants: Iranian Foreign Policy in the Rouhani Era," *Foreign Affairs*, April 17, 2014, https://www.foreignaffairs.com/articles/iran/2014-04-17/what-iran-really-wants.

[18]   Anoushiravan Ehteshami, "Islam as a Political Force in International Politics," in *Islam in World Politics*, ed. Nelly Lahoud and Anthony H. Johns (Abingdon, UK: Routledge, 2005), 29–53; Huntington, "The Clash of Civilizations?," 22–49.

[19]   Soumaya Ghannoushi, "Misconceptions of Political Islam," HuffPost, updated January 16, 2015, https://www.huffpost.com/entry/misconceptions-of-politic_b_6166086.

[20]   Warner and Walker, "Thinking About the Role of Religion in Foreign Policy."

[21]   J. David Singer, "The Level-of-Analysis Problem in International Relations," *World Politics* 14, no. 1 (October 1961): 77–92, https://doi.org/10.2307/2009557.

[22]   Valerie M. Hudson and Christopher S. Vore, "Foreign Policy Analysis Yesterday, Today, and Tomorrow," *Mershon International Studies Review* 39, no. 2 (October 1995): 209–238, https://doi.org/10.2307/222751; Warner and Walker, "Thinking About the Role of Religion in Foreign Policy."

[23]   Ben Child, "Ben Affleck: Sam Harris and Bill Maher 'Racist' and 'Gross' in Views of Islam," *Guardian*, October 7, 2014, http://www.theguardian.com/film/2014/oct/06/ben-affleck-bill-maher-sam-harris-islam-racist.

[24]   Mohammed Arkoun, "Rethinking Islam Today," *ANNALS of the American Academy of Political and Social Science* 588, no. 1 (2003): 18–39, https://doi.org/10.1177/0002716203588001003.

[25]   Diab, "The Invasion of Iraq and the Clash Within Civilizations."

PART III

GLOBAL INEQUALITY AND UNJUST VISIONS

CHAPTER VIII

PYGMÆOGERANOMACHIA OF IRANDOOST, OR THE POLITICS OF POSTCOLONIALISM

> "You never really understand a person until you consider things from his point of view—"
> "Sir?"
> "—until you climb into his skin and walk around in it."
>
> —Nelle Harper Lee, *To Kill a Mockingbird*

I had desired to become a special operations officer, for so long, that I was not much inclined to forego my amusement wish, which was a muddy mixture of ignorance and pride; an indifference to post-traumatic stress disorder which I did not know; a blind veneration of their training and exercises, like navigation, scuba diving, parachuting, survival, evasion, resistance, and escape (SERE) in arctic, desertic, jungled, mountainous, and oceanic environments; and a strong conviction of their moral right to conquest. After all that had been said of the military character of Daniel Craig's James Bond, as a former Special Air Service (SAS) type with expensive watches, I could not but believe that I could myself don by study and education a green beret on my head. The young Irandoost, who had determined not to lose the ambition of becoming a Royal Marine, then removed to the Special Boat Service (SBS), being almost wholly covered with thickets, like Lieutenant Commander Sam Fisher in a series of video games called *Tom Clancy's Splinter Cell*.

But this country (England), however it may delight all foreigners, except the French and their cultivated tongues, or the Scots and their skilled architects, philosophers, economists, doctors, and sociologists, who are among the artists considered masters of human judgment, is of no great advantage to the gazers, whose imaginations are not struck with the irreconcilable contrariety of classist modes of life, in which the discriminative men and women of the upper class do visibly treat the lower classes with contempt and abasement, in the manner by which the feudal scheme of polity has continued in Britain, "the Old Country." Whether the real manners of the neo-feudal lords are immediately perceived by a young multi-ethnic immigrant, like me, was not expected. For, till my dreams of adventure could be satisfied in Great Britain, before me, and on either side, lay the high mountains of Tabriz's Eynali in Iran and the Seven Hills of Iași in Romania, from which the eye ventured to look upon the Bannau Brycheiniog (Brecon Beacons).

But this is the age, in which those who have not read the history of their progenitors are easily persuaded to think that every improbable fiction of mass culture has been prepared for their voluntary entertainment in the artificial solitude and darkness of bedsits and gaming rooms, attended by a disfigured notion of self-sufficiency and an opiate indulgence in hasty delusions. The classist tenets of the national security establishments I was not curious to investigate, and they who through successive generations have always held unmeritoriously uncontested and unprincipled power, preserve hereditary prejudices sufficiently malignant and ignorant, because they operate upon the "surface truths" of life.[1] In consequence of this practice, the sons (Ethelbert, Josiah, Peregrine, Septimius, *et cetera, et cetera, et cetera*) and daughters (Griselda, Cressida, Euphemia, Tryphena, *et cetera, et cetera, et cetera*) of the higher families are fast-streamed into the top of the chain, after a voyage passed in the waste of uncultivated learning (decorated with the ornamental knowledge of *literae humaniores*) in the Eton Group and Oxbridge at full leisure, who then continue a vain scene of mediocre adventure in the armed forces, which pretend to the professional distinctions of rank and every claim of old royalist traditions, without the interruption of the *mauvaise honte* of an Englishman, preparing to while away their narrowness of life upon the labor of the hands of the poor and useless; a state of life to be variegated with artless commerce in the City of London and permanent vacations in their ill-treated French or Italian vineyards; they, I believe, are seduced by their vanity and wealth, in the Anglo-Saxon character.

Epistle I

When I had gone so far as to take possession of my passport as a naturalized citizen of the United Kingdom, I was granted the opportunity to make application to the Armed Forces, as a test of my pilgrimage to this occupied Brythonic, Pictish, and Goidelic land, which was almost ripe after my arrival at London Victoria nine years previously. This I did on the same day, yet I knew that the officer cadets of the Commando Training Centre Royal Marines (CTCRM), Royal Military Academy Sandhurst (RMAS), or Britannia Royal Naval College (BRNC) would go thither with accounts very different from mine. That the Old Etonian manners were continued where the ornamental Oxford English language was spoken, no variety of recruitment advertisements, containing the appearance of diversification and inclusivity, would have given me a more commodious view of the officers' mess; for I was not in danger of forgetting that in the film, *Lawrence of Arabia* (1962), very skillfully directed by Sir David Lean, a glass of lemonade was refused to Thomas Edward Lawrence who, after having loved "S. A." and drawn those tides of men into his hands and written his will across the sky in stars, had landed at the Cairo officers' club, though he (and his boyfriend) were dislodged with thirst.

Figure 8.1. Lawrence in Arabia in 1918, the mystery man of Saudi Arabia.

I was, without the right of appeal, or the proportion due to my merit, hindered in my advancement or progression (for which I am now thankful, as I will explain later), because the entrance had been stopped or guarded. I sent the next year a letter to a member of this Parliament, after a cessation of all intercourse from the recruitment center's correspondents for near three months, within which I wrote strong reasons to complain of that violent judicature; a few (redacted, for my own privacy) paragraphs used in this electronic particular, I think, may possibly storm with more force the heart of every reader.

> Dear . . . MP,
>
> As a constituent, I am writing a letter I never expected to compose. Anyway, please, allow me to explain that as a "multinational" man, it has nevertheless been my dream to join the British Army since I was . . . years old. However, even though I am nowadays a proud British passport holder and fully naturalized citizen, my application to join the Service as a Regular Officer has been rejected on the baseless ground I do not meet British citizenship criteria. A complete misinterpretation of my circumstances when considering I have repeatedly supplied each of the documents required. Facts eventually leading me to realize this process has been stained by blatant racism from the start of my application in . . . .
>
> Indeed, I should mention I first moved to London in . . . from Iran, having an Iranian father and Romanian mother, both of whom were eager to begin a new life in a country (Great Britain) where democracy was valued and people lived without persecution, or prejudice. Yet, my case has been completely mishandled from the outset, my questions dismissed, my concerns ignored and my every attempt to assist with documentation clearly repulsed in an almost cavalier fashion.
>
> Astonishingly, I frequently found myself chasing paperwork and Home Office guidelines in order to facilitate this process. Matters, of course, which needed to be undertaken by

professionals within the Army National Recruitment Centre itself. Afterwards, I was either greeted with total silence, or further extended delays, leading to illogical answers that always seemed to hover around my ethnicity. Astoundingly, I again immediately provided information from the Foreign Office regarding what can and cannot be done when dealing with the current Iranian regime, albeit to no avail.

Finally, I was rejected for completely contradictory reasons, accompanied by implied slurs on my racial background. What is more, every attempt to appeal against this decision appears to have been blocked by additional delays, along with unnecessarily lengthy silences. Everything above evidenced by either deliberately inconsistent feedback, or a tacit refusal to stop comparing my situation with applicants from the Commonwealth. In point of fact, my specific situation always fell on deaf ears.

Therefore, your intervention in this gross miscarriage of justice is essential, because little else will resolve my predicament.

Yours sincerely,

Daniele-Hadi Irandoost FRSA

Yet I received such rehearsed answers as, till the outbreak of the coronavirus disease 2019 (COVID-19) had put a stop to all communication with those who were stationed to subdue my official complaint, that it made me acquainted with colonialist manners, and showed how many unaltered indiscriminations may be conglobated into one ignorant and mean idea, by the grossest help of incestuous or hereditary bigotry. I could not but be conscious that my migrant's face was exposed to the rudeness of the clonal financial classes in the autonomous City of London, where bankers and psychos are in great numbers errand boys to the richest families or the "shadow elite,"[2] and among whose innumerable faults, to extend our speculation, piratical avarice (with a vigilance of jealousy) may be reasonably supposed.

Epistle II

From this I inferred, that the grammar of my destiny was not the grammar of the establishment in Great Britain,[3] and I no longer deceived myself by a false opinion of their moral sanctity. This I perceived as something unexpected, because I knew that, when they thought it preferable to any monetary expense, they would be willing to turn aside their eyes and conscience, which to the unprejudiced John le Carré appeared thusly,

> To one innocent dead woman . . . nothing.
> To one innocent dead child . . . nothing.
> To one soldier who did his duty . . . disgrace.
> To one retired diplomat . . . a knighthood.[4]

The people of that little community precluded the "other" from contact or sympathy, and were accustomed to endure their little wants, like Aldous Leonard Huxley's narcotic soma in *Brave New World*, which David William Parry has so often recommended to my notice, more than to remove them— not unlike that in Eric Arthur Blair's *Nineteen Eighty-Four*. It seemed that the mixture of my "colored" genealogy and the want of money had raised dislike; I was gentle and pleasing, but not the son of Count Bobolescue or Lady Fortescue; no artificial masks could be worn, nor could I form any alliances within the precincts of the golden triangle of privilege.[5] I had made my way, after several years at Aberystwyth University in Wales and earning three academical degrees in intelligence studies and the public profession of teaching, to zero-hour contract employment in teaching English as a foreign language (TEFL) and supply teaching, which were all that I was entitled to claim.

The Design

In the middle of the COVID-19 pandemic, at the time when I and the bard who so easily saturates my soul with love songs were preparing to register as civil partners, I was glad of our arrival at Mu Mu Land, because I knew that the mistaken conviction of my first intention would have undersold the general measure of my abilities and attainments, and reduced them to nothing. The official complaints were not pursued; yet I had now felt an unexpected emersion from darkness into light, in which I, unlike Number Six in Patrick McGoohan's *The Prisoner*, obtained the victory, and Number One, with his surveilled mysterious coastal village, was defeated and repulsed: nor did I interest myself in working on the neo-colonialist and imperialist institutions that operate upon subaltern lives globally and nationally, like the Circus (MI6) in Vauxhall, the Doughnut (Government Communications Headquarters, GCHQ) in Cheltenham, or Box 500 (MI5) in Millbank. These agencies, I am afraid, have directly and formally betrayed the traditional liberal foundations that made this a nation once progressive, which the births of William Shakespeare, John Locke, John Stuart Mill, Adam Smith, David Hume, and the "intellectual aristocracy" consisting of the Darwins, the Huxleys, the Wedgwoods, the Tates, and the Stephens, *et cetera*, allotted it.[6]

Figure 8.2. Portmeirion, the location for the television show, *The Prisoner*.

Such were the reflections that this anxious and toilsome journey had given me an opportunity of seeing, and such were the things which decolonial sight had raised. Of the rank or understanding of a colonized people, I probably had attained such knowledge or general experience as might justly be admitted in the traditional history of abolitionist movements, but which had doubtless been imagined by English Dissenters, like the Quakers, the Ranters, the Levellers, the Diggers, the Swedenborgians, the Unitarians, the Methodists, the Congregationalists, *et cetera, et cetera*. This tradition is very properly mentioned by the Rev. Dr. Parry, the Catholic minister who authored an esoteric journey from the Druidic precipice of Albion to the Eastern Orthodox precipice of holy Mount Athos.[7] Since I was the treasurer for the Rev. Dr. Parry's licensed chapel, called by LGBTQIA+ assemblies as St. Valentine's Hall, I was glad when he, with what stores of imagery, and with what principles of conception, and by stretching my understanding wider and wider, informed me of the distinctions among these separate congregations.

It need not, I suppose, be mentioned, ze (gender-neutral neopronoun) that has often suffered the violence of real physical or psychological racism, will find in Dr. Frantz Omar Fanon's *Black Skin, White Masks* a useful companion to hir (another gender-neutral neopronoun) life.[8] Like the Martinicans in their diminished state, after several centuries of colonial, rustic rule under the superintendence of a brutal colonial police, described by that Black Jacobin (Fanon), I began to think about the worst effect of the upper class, inclining many to suspect, that they could give it good examples of elegance—*like whited sepulchers, which indeed appear beautiful outward, but are within full of dead men's bones, and of all uncleanness*—only because it seemed such qualities were necessary to climb the rugged social ascent. I, being thus deprived of the universal right of dignity, as my divine birth right, was required to possess the same value as other colored subalterns.

The Descent of Dullness

A decent attempt, as I was told at Aberystwyth, was made to convert postcolonial politics into a kind of universal justice, which could hardly fail to extend the benefits of equal liberality to the lowest ranks of people. Professor Robert J. C. Young, in his book *Postcolonialism: A Very Short Introduction*, informed us that the aim of postcolonial politics is to overturn the general frame of our thoughts, so that whoever surveys the world must see things from the windows, the frames of which are in the eye or imagination of the Other.[9] This closely resembles the *bildungsroman* narrative of *To Kill a Mockingbird*, written with vigor by the Methodist author Nelle Harper Lee, eminently adapted to impress upon bigoted minds the sanctity of compassion, or the impulse of empathy.[10] We are told on a very memorable occasion towards the end of the novel that Jean Louise "Scout" Finch tried to put herself in the shoes of Arthur "Boo" Radley (a white recluse who is compared with totally defenseless, unarmed, innocent mockingbirds), knowing she was neither superior to nor inferior to the common people in importance. For, considered in itself, having any experience of a stranger's streams of life will annex the language of hir "particular" philosophical, poetical, historical, social, cultural, and linguistic stories to the fundamental (or spiritual) superstructure of our essence, which is undoubtedly equally distributed:[11] and even the balance of dissimilar "particulars" is so intricate as to enhance the similitude of appearance, as Edward Wadie Said has remarked in *Culture and Imperialism*: "No one today is purely *one* thing" (italics in the original).[12]

We are so (noumenally) equal, notwithstanding the accidental difference of background, race, language, religion, gender, sexuality, that there is no apparent reason for imputing more power to one person over another. To expand the human race to its full perfection, it seems necessary that the mind be decolonized by an intellectual retrogradation, which decenters the rays of Western knowledge from a focus. But so much of the world's problems are still frozen in deep wells, that a very scanty short term solution must not overwhelm any structural change that overmatches the "prevailing order."[13] Foucault observed in his account of the oppression of the disciplinary institution in our modern nation states, such as asylums, schools, prisons, army barracks, and factories are, that the oppressive relations may be broken by the interposition of some superstructural treatment,[14] which improves not merely mundane appearances or artificial modes of life, but yields nothing less than the great effects of systemic processes.[15] There is still extant, in the books of Ibrahim (Omar Fanon's *nom de guerre*), an unaccustomed degree of found personal experience, whose "subjective" or "particular" views gave opportunity for a revival of a global movement that hoped to recover the independence of the ex-colonies from the seat of colonial rule, and, therefore, nullify the "prevailing order." Among an oppressed people, the natural product of personal hardship, to which they are exposed, bears the consciousness of postcolonial politics.

Fall of Colonialism

One day I found some novels on a shelf, among which was an edition of Kurt Vonnegut's *Slaughterhouse-Five or the Children's Crusade: A Duty-Dance with Death*, which reminded me that my goals had "died away," but were restocked by a nobler chorus of the exalting musick of ambition; and "so it goes."[16] Postcolonial politics has now become one of the favorite studies of academical institutions in the English-speaking world. How far teachers have happened to succeed in the decolonization of curriculums in universities, it is not easy to know. However, I am persuaded that postcolonialism is a subject of philosophical curiosity that illuminates the relation between instruments of violence (by way of armed forces), and the outrages, as well as oppressions, that preserve the imperialist genealogies and the status quo in the international relations of Western and non-Western countries. I find also that the art of self-criticism, accompanied by the Catholic phrase *mea culpa*, is variously encompassed by the multifarious obligation co-operated by decolonial thinking and practice for the purpose of hindering the ignorance of hypocrisy, self-righteousness, and censoriousness, that would readily importune me with inquiries about remedies for the unequal balance of power relations between two countries, and what criticism my translation of decolonial politics, that is, expedients intending to banish spiritual inequality like the ladies and gentlemen of the Clapham Sect (or the Clapham Saints), would produce. Decoloniality is likely to be multiplied by the epidemical encouragement of all strangers, who, finding themselves before, converse with the culture of other lands, the traditions of other peoples (though they may appear to them like beings of another world!), and the distinctions of religious ceremony, and, in peace, intercourse with the unconditional influx of new sources of inner riches, which history has extensively diversified by now. That is why I still put significant effort into learning British and other languages and cultures. I praise the travels and literary labors of Marco Polo, Sir Patrick Leigh Fermor, Ibn Battuta, Charles Robert Darwin, Jules Gabriel Verne, and the Rev. David William Parry, whose acute observations help any future traveler to pass from the gloom of the idle project of a young head to hir coalition with hir fellows, which would perhaps often make everybody communicative and empower their strength of human judgment. According to these schemes, peace quickly begins when the world is inhabited by those who consider another not as "an object in the midst of other objects,"[17] but as a universal end in hirself.

ENDNOTES

[1] David William Parry, *Women in Mayhem: Or Three Nonsensical Pranks* (Melbourne: Manticore Press, 2024), 13.

[2] Janine R. Wedel, *Shadow Elite: How the World's New Power Brokers Undermine Democracy, Government, and the Free Market* (New York: Basic Books, 2009).

[3] Liberally, the "grammar of my destiny" is a slight alteration of the title of David William Parry's second collection of poems, *The Grammar of Witchcraft* (Hemel Hempstead, UK: Hertfordshire Press, 2016).

[4] David William Parry gifted John le Carré's *A Delicate Truth* (London: Penguin Books, 2014), on my birthday.

[5] I borrowed the names of Count Bobolescue and Lady Fortescue, with which Michael Bentine furnished the sketch comedy "The Toast Master," which David William Parry introduced me to.

[6] David William Parry, *Mount Athos Inside Me: Essays on Religion, Swedenborg and Arts* (Melbourne: Manticore Press, 2019), 225.

[7] Parry, *Mount Athos Inside Me*, 209.

[8] Frantz Fanon, *Black Skin, White Masks*, trans. Charles Lam Markmann (London: Pluto, 1986).

[9] Robert J. C. Young, *Postcolonialism: A Very Short Introduction* (Oxford: Oxford University Press, 2003), 6–8.

[10] Harper Lee, *To Kill a Mockingbird* (London: Heinemann Educational, 1966).

[11] Naeem Inayatullah, "Falling and Flying: An Introduction," In *Autobiographical International Relations: I, IR*, ed. Naeem Inayatullah (Abingdon, UK: Routledge, 2011), 8.

[12] Edward Said, *Culture and Imperialism* (New York: Vintage Books, 1994), 336.

[13] Maja Zehfuss, "Conclusion: What Can We Do to Change the World?," in *Global Politics: A New Introduction*, ed. Jenny Edkins and Maja Zehfuss (Abingdon, UK: Routledge, 2014), 624.

[14] Michel Foucault, *Power/Knowledge: Selected Interviews and Other Writings 1972-1977*, ed. Colin Gordon, trans. Colin Gordon and Others (New York: Pantheon Books, 1980).

[15] Frantz Fanon, *The Wretched of the Earth*, preface by Jean-Paul Sartre, trans. Constance Farrington (New York: Grove Press, 1963).

[16] Kurt Vonnegut, Jr. *Slaughterhouse Five or the Children's Crusade: A*

Duty-Dance with Death (London: Vintage, 1991).

[17]   Fanon, *Black Skin, White Masks*, 109.

CHAPTER IX

OF COLONIALISM AND GLOBAL INEQUALITIES

When we two meet, we meet like rushing torrents;
Like warring winds, like flames from various points,
That mate each other's fury—there is naught
Of elemental strife, were fiends to guide it,
Can match the wrath of man.

—André Frénaud

Colonialism, until the American revolutionary armies broke silence, was the emblem of the imperial cause at the four corners of the worldly stage. The course of centuries has well-nigh elapsed since the series of events which took place in North America. Thus the glow of reviving hope ran on, and in that vein decolonization has long continued. The collection of works of fiction and non-fiction that contains the outlines of the history of colonized nations and colonizing empires, are carefully preserved in the intelligentsia's library apparently filled with books and manuscripts, or the revolutionary's street poster-ed and barricaded with carts. On entering the library, or study, and ascending a short stair, they find themselves with a treasure by the fireside, pluck it in their bosom and, having proclaimed silence, open the proceedings by reading the following rhymes:

> Turning and turning in the widening gyre
> The falcon cannot hear the falconer;
> Things fall apart; the centre cannot hold;
> Mere anarchy is loosed upon the world.

And so reciting, Albert Chinụalụmọgụ Achebe laid the opening of his novel, and called it *Things Fall Apart*.[1] The young Nigerian seemed closely to scrutinize his own social thews and cultural sinews that he had hitherto witnessed in Igboland, over which the white man exercised domination by guns that never shot. Achebe was the first to express his sense of impropriety in suffering the deeply wicked injustice of his own country's material and psychological inequalities, refusing to let them remain obscured in gloom.

This opinion is confirmed both by documentary evidence and by contemporary historians. And if we examine the proceedings of the present global scene, we shall see that, in principle, there is essentially no difference whatever between the richest few, or "global elite," as they are called, who "share a combined wealth of £1tn, as much as the poorest 3.5 billion of the world's population,"[2] and the bonds of colonialism on the banks of the Niger River.

In the meantime, the thought suddenly bursts on our mind: here is no angel of punishment that marshals the poor on a path of retribution—here the half-starved herds keep their eyes riveted on the mainour of their avaricious extortioners who, marked by assumed superiority and presumption, willfully prevent any foray of their worthless subjects from reaching seigniorial pasturage. I shake my head, and I too say, there is something in all this that I understand not, and will seek to understand. Perhaps if I have good fortune in my attempts to review the rich stores of postcolonial literature, divided betwixt the exertions of modernization theory and underdevelopment theory, I can lay down an explanation of the cause.

"Speak on, but be brief," says the social justice warrior in red, "and know, you (a pompous ass) speak to one whose resolution cannot be melted with your eloquence." Know then, I say, that modernization theory suggests that underdevelopment in poor countries exists because of the attitude assumed by their people, as well as the whole structural system of the country, rather than because of the historical relations which stand betwixt themselves and the developed world.[3] On the other hand, underdevelopment theory conjectures, that the descendants of the historical relations between the colonized and the colonizer, and the economic system of the evil spirit of the subterranean dungeon of Mammon, might best express the nature of the offence.[4] I then exclaim anew: so, if your cavaliers will permit, I will forward and examine the two sides of the stream, which might render intelligible to us the necessity of such a course of politics. I also hope to consider the theory said to have kindled a spark of light, which Karl Marx threw upon the matter, and held with known and notorious publicity in the open air. A singular circumstance that led to the broad stream itself, hurrying forward with dizzy rapidity, and shaking the gates of the upper class's castle as by a whirlwind; and a collective voice was heard to demand the common ownership of material resources due to their comrades. Either way, let us see what is the meaning of "colonialism" and "global inequality," before we determine what is the connection betwixt them.

The Definition, Drawn and Etched

Britannica describes colonialism as a "political-economic phenomenon whereby various European nations explored, conquered, settled, and exploited large areas of the world."[5] The reader who would wish to examine with attention the historical events that gave rise to such a change will find known examples at the end of the fifteenth century—that important period, in which peripatetic mariners discovered, through new sea routes, the key to the southern coast of Africa (1488) and the Americas (1492), which augured that sea power had shifted "from the Mediterranean to the Atlantic and to the emerging nation-states of Portugal, Spain, the Dutch Republic, France, and England."[6] Composedly stated, global inequality relates to social or economic inequality on a planetary level, though I will take occasion hereafter to focus on economic inequality between and within all countries.

The Duel, Drawn and Etched

The theory of underdevelopment intrudes upon some trying questions which occupy the minds of those who have no claim to obtain any share of the benefits of their labor. Sankaran Krishna asks whether it was "a coincidence that the rising prosperity and affluence of a handful of nations in the West occurred during the same centuries as the conquest of the New World and the colonization of Asia and Africa?"[7] When the question was intimated to Andre Gunder Frank, he returned an answer, in a calm and even tone of voice, in which the German guttural sounds were calculatingly intermixed: "contemporary underdevelopment is in large part zee historical product of past und continuing economic und ozer relazions betveen zatellite underdeveloped und zee now developed metropolitan countries."[8] He adds, that history can impart to the reader some examples so completely as to show the incapacitating effects often produced by colonialism in all Latin American countries, and of which the Republic of Chile and the Federative Republic of Brazil had, as Frank well knew, their full share. Undoubtedly, in Brazil, "Zee expansion of zee vorld economy since zee beginning of zee zixteenth century successively converted zee Northeast, zee Minas Gerais interior, zee North, und zee Center-South (Rio de Janeiro, São Paulo, und Paraná) into export economies und incorporated zem into zee structure und development of zee vorld capitalist zystem."[9] Still, although the region underwent "economic development during zee period of its respective golden age . . . zee market or zee productivity of zee first three regions declined, foreign und domestic economic interest in zem vaned; und zey vere left to develop zee underdevelopment zey live today."[10] This is elucidated by a note of Krishna's: "The emergence of the idea of private property in land . . . converted the Latin American countryside into giant landed estates, or *latifundias*, producing cash crops and livestock for export to Europe rather than for the needs of domestic society."[11] So saying, he recalls the use of "coercive forms of labor organization, including slavery . . . precluded the rise of democratic or individualistic values";[12] at the same time, taking a view of the "elitist character of the domestic market and the imposition of free trade," he comes to the conclusion, that "the Latin American colonies imported their manufactured goods from Europe rather than manufacturing them locally."[13] In a word, the underdevelopment theory attests to the extraverted growth (a feature of colonialism) which characterized the underdevelopment of Latin America.[14]

According to the historical evidence on which it rests, as Krishna says, "Those parts able to resist the political, economic, and social domination of England and other early industrializers were able to join them as developed societies in due time, and those that could not were invariably colonized and underdeveloped as a result."[15] In truth, the unification of the Thirteen Colonies, which formed the United States of America (USA), serves as an example of unconquered courage that "asserted their political and economic sovereignty from England on the issue of imposed free trade" and laid the foundation for a colonized people's independence.[16] For that matter, also, I am reminded of the road which the young Communists pursued, under the guidance of the party, until at length they withdrew themselves from the flames of colonialism that pertained to the Russian Empire, and emerged at once into liberty and great consequence; the Union of Soviet Socialist Republics (USSR) found a place accordingly next to the USA, as a superpower should have done. And, contrary to the doctrines of modernization theory, some visible experience indicates that in underdeveloped countries economic development may be easily supposed without taking the slightest notice of most "relations of diffusion."[17]

Indeed, Marx saw beneath colonialism (the singular expression of imperialism) one of the implements of capitalism, which aided in raising the profits of the upper stratum of society, who gained their existence through cheating the indigenous people of colonized lands. In fact, the German-born philosopher, in common with many of his representatives, would have been alarmed by the habits of colonialism, this most unexpected obstacle to the liberation of the "working class" from the conquests and ambitions of the upper class. In their *Manifesto of the Communist Party*, Marx and Friedrich Engels had already noticed that "the need of a constantly expanding market for its products chases the bourgeoisie over the whole surface of the globe."[18] Colonialism was adjudged "as a major moment in the historical process of" so-called primitive accumulation, and thus "as a precondition for the domination of the capitalist mode of production (CMP)."[19] Indeed, Marx was convinced that "the colonial system ripened, like a hot-house, trade and navigation. . . . The treasures captured outside Europe by undisguised looting, enslavement, and murder, floated back to the mother country and were turned into capital."[20]

For this purpose, colonialism elevates the Leviathan who stretches and yawns portentously for its monopolistic colonial economy. There was so much consequence to the guarantee of honorable commerce in this iniquitous conduct, that Adam Smith was diametrically "opposed to the exclusive (monopolistic) trade conditions which the mother countries established with their colonies."[21] This was peculiarly the case with the capital of Kenya, which "was appropriated from the African population through primitive accumulation (land alienation and forced labour) and through wage labour" by the exactions and violence levied by English oppressors.[22] And it appears that the International Labour Organization (ILO) mission in Kenya revealed the inquisitorial findings of investigations conducted in 1972. It was reported that there was "a fundamental 'imbalance' of the economy" between "the working poor" and those few who "enjoyed highly rewarding employment."[23] It was no difficult matter for the Swiss mission to impute this phenomenon "to the fact that at independence the colonial economy had been taken over largely intact, and that this economy had been structured to yield high incomes for the small white minority; and it also pointed out that the school system, the pattern of government spending, the fiscal and tax system, investment policy, and so on, reinforced this economic structure."[24] It is only in this manner that Kenya, in a situation of helpless adversity, escaped from the ruined prison of colonialism and now stands on the precarious drawbridge of neocolonialism, one near the mouth of a subterranean abyss, at the bottom of which a neoliberal torrent surges and boils with unabated fury. It might therefore be expected "that ex-colonies and developing countries are still subordinated to imperialist countries through dependency relations."[25] It bears little to add that "a special type of development of the countries dependent on imperialism is characteristic of the international capitalist division of labor within the framework of the world capitalist system. The dependence created by colonialism is still manifested in all the key spheres of the developing countries' economic life";[26] while the spread of European institutions and structural systems in the colonies showed, "these metropolis-satellite relations are not limited to the imperial or international level but penetrate and structure the very economic, political, and social life" of the developed countries.[27]

The Examination, Drawn and Etched

Fixed, therefore, in purpose, neo-liberalism ventures to split politics and economics in twain, and render the latter a private matter, just beyond the point at which the state had previously occupied. Perhaps it is owing to this vision that the state is prevented from interfering in economic affairs, in order to redistribute wealth amongst the poor. This modernizing practice has its origin in the age of modern colonialism, which mingled with and enhanced capitalism. The received ideas of Smith combined to recommend competitiveness and inner individual creativity for the benefit of economic development.[28] These were almost similarly maintained by Walt Whitman Rostow, in *The Stages of Economic Growth: A Non-Communist Manifesto*, who thus testified to the five stages of economic growth through which any country progressively passes upwards, like a person who grows to become an adult.[29] Accordingly, he grounded his thoughts in national independence, and thought, of course, that underdeveloped countries could achieve the distinguished success which would place them upon the same footing upon which all developed countries seemed to have placed their intercourse.[30] This ahistorical model indicates that "poorer nations have largely themselves to blame for not making the transition."[31] It was not the first time it was suspected that the "dual" societies and economies of underdeveloped countries were independent of each other within their districts. In few words, the better part of their country was deemed the more likely to be in contact with the "outside" world;[32] whereas the other was "widely regarded as variously isolated, subsistence-based, feudal, or precapitalist, and therefore more underdeveloped."[33] This sentiment was so prominent, that it poured its Eurocentric streams of mist into the vicinage of modernization theory, by which, it generally contends that global inequalities in the world are not to be explained by colonialism.

Yet let me retort, with something of a scrutinizing glance at modernization theory—the very act levels distinctions betwixt global inequality and colonialism; because the theory does not satisfactorily account for the fact that capitalism can simultaneously generate development and underdevelopment, whether of high or low degree. We have also reason to think that members of this school of thought may be ignorant of the historical cycles that nations go through, and do not always spring lightly from the root of underdevelopment to the stem of development. For this reason, although it was the most natural arrangement, where a developed country was conceived to be "underdeveloped" in the initial stages of capitalism, such countries were not underdeveloped—in truth "they may have been *un*developed" (italics in the original).[34] But, above all, the school of thought associated with underdevelopment theory draws on a considerable portion of historical events in Asia, Africa, Latin America, etc., confirming the idea that global inequality had its origin in colonialism.

The Conclusion, Drawn and Etched

To conclude, in so serious an affair, can the close connection between global inequality and colonialism be really admitted? I have attended to answer the question as briefly as the other chapters. This, I have labored to answer; and, thereupon, I have heard with the ears and seen with the eyes of Marx. I recollected that modernization theory differentiates global inequality from colonialism as mutually exclusive phenomena. "Capitalist colonialism," quoth Krishna, "has rendered our understanding of the world Eurocentric, and we are unable to think outside the categories and concepts that emerged in post–Columbian Europe."[35] Hence, to those who speculate upon the invigorating effect of free trade or liberalization on regional, national, and international inequalities, we are determined at once to give a view of the opposite side; only, that, by the abstraction of "capitalist colonialism and its contemporary manifestations everywhere, we can begin to understand and reverse its effects and embark on human development."[36] Here, in the course of surveying the wonted intercourse of colonialism, capitalism, imperialism, etc., I have been enabled to express a sense of their connection with global inequality.

ENDNOTES

[1]   Chinua Achebe, *Things Fall Apart* (London: Heinemann Educational, 1971).

[2]   Graeme Wearden, "Oxfam: 85 Richest People as Wealthy as Poorest Half of the World," *Guardian*, January 20, 2014, https://www.theguardian.com/business/2014/jan/20/oxfam-85-richest-people-half-of-the-world.

[3]   Sankaran Krishna, *Globalization and Postcolonialism: Hegemony and Resistance in the Twenty-First Century* (Plymouth, UK: Rowman and Littlefield Publishers, 2009).

[4]   Krishna, *Globalization and Postcolonialism.*

[5]   Richard A. Webster et al., "Western Colonialism," in *Encyclopaedia Britannica*, April 11, 2025, https://www.britannica.com/topic/Western-colonialism.

[6]   Webster et al., "Western Colonialism."

[7]   Krishna, *Globalization and Postcolonialism*, 16.

[8]   Andre Gunder Frank, "The Development of Underdevelopment (1969)," in *The Globalization and Development Reader: Perspectives on Development and Global Change*, 2nd ed., ed. J. Timmons Roberts, Amy Bellone Hite, and Nitsan Chorev (Chichester, UK: Wiley-Blackwell, 2015), 106.

[9]   Frank, "The Development of Underdevelopment (1969)," 108.

[10]   Frank, "The Development of Underdevelopment (1969)," 108.

[11]   Krishna, *Globalization and Postcolonialism*, 17.

[12]   Krishna, *Globalization and Postcolonialism*, 17.

[13]   Krishna, *Globalization and Postcolonialism*, 17.

[14]   Krishna, *Globalization and Postcolonialism*, 17.

[15]   Krishna, *Globalization and Postcolonialism*, 27.

[16]   Krishna, *Globalization and Postcolonialism*, 27.

[17]   Frank, "The Development of Underdevelopment (1969)," 106.

[18]   Karl Marx and Friedrich Engels, "Manifesto of the Communist Party (1948) and Alienated Labour (1844)," in *The Globalization and Development Reader: Perspectives on Development and Global Change*, 2nd ed., ed. J. Timmons Roberts, Amy Bellone Hite, and Nitsan Chorev (Chichester, UK: Wiley-Blackwell, 2015), 31.

[19]   John Milios, "Colonialism and Imperialism: Classic Texts," in *Encyclopedia of Political Economy*, vol. 1: A–K, ed. Phillip Anthony O'Hara (London: Routledge, 1998), 114.

[20] Karl Marx, *The Process of Production of Capital*, vol. 1 of *Capital: A Critique of Political Economy*, trans. Samuel Moore and Edward Aveling from the 3rd German ed., ed. Friedrich Engels, revised and amplified according to the 4th German ed. by Ernest Untermann (Moscow: Progress Publishers, n.d.), 826.

[21] Milios, "Colonialism and Imperialism," 113.

[22] Colin Leys, *Underdevelopment in Kenya: The Political Economy of Neo-Colonialism 1964–1971* (Nairobi, Kenya: East African Education Publishers, 1975), 254.

[23] Leys, *Underdevelopment in Kenya*, 258.

[24] Leys, *Underdevelopment in Kenya*, 259.

[25] Milios, "Colonialism and Imperialism," 116.

[26] Yuri Popov, *Essays in Political Economy: Imperialism and the Developing Countries* (Moscow: Progress Publishers, 1984), 119, quoted in Milios, "Colonialism and Imperialism," 116.

[27] Frank, "The Development of Underdevelopment (1969)," 107.

[28] Adam Smith, *An Inquiry into the Nature and Causes of the Wealth of Nations*, with an introduction by Mark G. Spencer (Ware, UK: Wordsworth Editions, 2012).

[29] W. W. Rostow, *The Stages of Economic Growth: A Non-Communist Manifesto*, 3rd ed. (Cambridge: Cambridge University Press, 1990).

[30] Krishna, *Globalization and Postcolonialism*, 13.

[31] Krishna, *Globalization and Postcolonialism*, 14.

[32] Frank, "The Development of Underdevelopment (1969)," 106.

[33] Frank, "The Development of Underdevelopment (1969)," 106.

[34] Frank, "The Development of Underdevelopment (1969)," 18.

[35] Krishna, *Globalization and Postcolonialism*, 29.

[36] Krishna, *Globalization and Postcolonialism*, 29.

CHAPTER X

GLOBAL ECONOMIC GOVERNANCE:
ON SOME TECHNICAL ELEMENTS OF GLOBALIZATION AND THE
INCREASE OF WEALTH AND ECONOMIC GROWTH IN HISTORICALLY
MARGINALIZED DEVELOPING COUNTRIES

> When I hae a saxpence under my thumb,
> Then I get credit in ilka town;
> But when I am puir they bid me gae by—
> Oh, poverty parts good company!

—Sir Walter Scott, *The Abbot*

Such as it is, economic globalization is described by scholarly fellows as the process by which the economy of a country is gradually integrated into the global economy through the combined removal of barriers, the deregulation of the market (i.e., open and free markets), and the liberalization of trade, and so forth. In this, as in other matters, the neoliberal policies of Mrs. Thatcher and Mr. Reagan, since the latter part of the 1970s, accelerated the pace of globalization by supporting the cause of privatization, deregulation, free markets, etc. The proponents of globalization generally aver that the plantation of these programs in developing countries are sufficient to enable them to emerge through the history of their marginalized economic and political conditions. "Globalisation theory," suggests Kiely, in part at least, "constitutes a neoliberal version of modernization theory."[1] However, what I have hinted at is not without some previous criticism. Indeed, we have seen recently the breathings of anti-globalizing antagonists and post-colonial theorists who have blown the sparks of social movements into the rebellious flames of Orc; and it can scarce be doubted that the act of violence on the Twin Towers in New York City on September 11, 2001, was driven by the perpetrators' extreme aversion to this process.

Figure 10.1. A worker during the construction of the Empire State Building.

I now interrupt this prolegomena, in order to announce my desire to debate these things pro and con, and in the pursuit of this matter, I have formed a resolution, of which, if I may presume to share some particulars, you will find the general result in this chapter. In this I am compelled to judge of the processes and active agents—international financial institutions such as the International Monetary Fund (IMF), the World Bank, and the World Trade Organization (WTO)—in the course of globalization. With these questions pressed on my mind, I have taken the liberty to divide my answer to them between four parts, occupying a dozen or so good pages of paper. The first part, being an argumentation—impressed by the seven-leagued boots of the ogre Kapital—would be transcribed by the adherents of globalization. The second of these parts contains a review of the annals of literature, apparently suspicious of the excess of globalization, that, with a sort of desperate attempt to disarm the discourse of their antagonists, reverberate again and again and again on sleeping ears, like rival thunder through the multiplied rebounding echoes of a bare cliff. It is seen in the third the sketch of critical remarks upon such actors as the IMF and the WTO that have given globalization scope for exertion. But chiefly and above all the rest, my own inference forms the last subject of my blotted paper. I conclude, then, that globalization and any party partial to the cause of extensive and increasing trade with the Third World cannot, strictly speaking, relieve those whole countries from the sufferings of their filth and their poverty to which they are attached.

The Globalizing Expedition

I have already said that those who stand in the exterior circle, with their faces to the "Gemini City,"[2] and their backs to those inner citadels which the unconquerable poet the Rev. David William Parry has so often described, aver that a free and open global economy can remove any acknowledged difficulty faced by people in the developing world. On inquiry, we find that this policy of pushing on the open market is judged to lay the foundation of wealth and prosperity, which, if endured with patience and steadiness, may in time coming inspire the children of those against whom the acts of colonial exploitation had been directed with courage to ascend from their powerless *paupera regna*, in their darkened Wellsian caverns, and spring into the broad daylight.

There is, accordingly, a kind of correspondence between the proceedings of globalization and the direct alleviation of poverty;[3] because neo-liberalizing policies, as they contrive to achieve the truth of what they affirm, offer competition, increase the flow of capital, investment, efficiency, innovation and give effect to trickle-down economics, so that, considering the labyrinth of mercantile speculation, they can contribute to the wealth of all.[4] Professor Arie Kacowicz of the Hebrew University of Jerusalem's description of the subject may be here quoted—

> The liberal view of global economic relationships, which is based on "mutual" (even "complex") interdependence, regards international economic relationships between developed and developing countries as mutually beneficial and benign. In this view, the forces of globalization will eventually stimulate

economic growth in the developing nations, thus reducing and even eradicating poverty by allowing the forces of the market to play themselves out without any state intervention.[5]

Robert Wade, who is within hearing, observes, "when a high cost, high wage, high saving economy (A) interacts through free markets with a low cost, low wage, low saving economy (B), capital tends to move from A to B in search of higher returns, and labour from B to A."[6]

And to back this promissory prospect of extrication from the acknowledged difficulties of their situation, international institutions, like the World Bank, have been engaged in many of the statistical accounts of the accomplishments of globalization. For example, an estimate assembled by the World Bank presented its findings as follows: "In 2011, 17 percent of people in the developing world lived at or below $1.25 a day. That's down from 43 percent in 1990 and 52 percent in 1981."[7] International financial institutions (IFIs) conceive it likely, therefore, that the People's Republic of China (PRC) and the Republic of India have had eminent success in their attempts to withdraw poverty from the sum of human existence, among the lower classes of their respective populations, a result attributed, it is said, to their strict and rigorous compliance with the terms of trade agreements.

What is more, it may be observed, that notwithstanding the apparent failure, and even impossibility, of the unconscientious schemes of neoliberalism in most developing countries, IFIs continue to exhort and encourage their *protégés*, so to speak, to pursue the dictates of an open economy, while intimating, insofar as their earlier works merited, that the gradual extension of the sphere of the private sector is presumed to create a great deal more employment.[8] In short, this view of the matter is tinged with the idea, derived from the principles of modernization theory, that developing countries occupy the elementary part of the high road to that terrestrial paradise (i.e., the final stage of Whig historiography), distinguished by materialistic acquirements, whether mass production or consumption.

Indeed, as I had learned from Whitfield, by second hand, the difference and distinction between the measure of development in the Global North and that of the Global South was engendered by the main strength of the Industrial Revolution in Britain;[9] at the same time the Global South was impeded in its progress by the shades of authoritarian regimes, ineffective state institutions, incomplete liberalization, and so forth. An American politician makes a bare statement of the contrast betwixt the civilized mode of life on the one side of the Brandt Line, and the uncultivated sort of life which is followed on the opposite side of that boundary: "Markets are an expression of the deepest truths about human nature and . . . as a result, they will ultimately be correct."[10] Upon the whole, therefore, we are disposed to think, that developing countries are less likely to attain the benefits from the promiscuous scene of globalization.

Figure 10.2. Hong Kong at night. View from Hong Kong Baptist University.

The Black Stone of Globalization

It is IFIs' opinion that neoliberalism is a force sufficient to procure the most important objects of globalization. The reader will find this particular fact illustrated in the neoliberal machinations of Western-educated economists, who, as before mentioned, steadfastly asserted the truth of what they had before affirmed; in a word, despite the collapse of the global economy in 2007–2008 in consequence of the short-sighted practices of neoliberalism and globalization, they urged all financial institutions to tread the same path of liberalization, and even spoke of exercising this encroachment on a more extended scale.[11] Nevertheless, their view has been criticized in late years, and, as it is well founded in post-Keynesianism, it has been insisted that capitalism is contradictory. It is plain, from the circumstances attending laissez-faire, that in one respect it lowers the price of primary goods because of the formal inclination of capitalist competition to decrease "prospective yield, and correspondingly the marginal efficiency of capital."[12] And really, under these disadvantages, the developing world exports primary goods only, while the volatile price of such primary goods as were found in the oil crises was of benefit to the neighbors in the Global North, instead of the oil-rich developing countries that produced raw materials. Hence, in spite of all propensities which form as it were the decrees of globalization, the long-term export of their primary goods is unlikely to bring in gains for exporters, on account of the regular depletion of resources, while their importers in the industrialized world focus on skill-intensive industries that generate higher returns.[13] At any rate, it means that low prices precipitate slow or no growth for most developing nations.

What is more, another self-contradiction in neoliberalism relates to the issue of income inequality. At length, Nuno Martins ejaculates, by way of summing up:

> Contrarily to what is often assumed in orthodox economic theory ... an increase in savings will not necessarily lead to a lower interest rate or higher investment, since in post-Keynesian theory the interest rate is determined by the level of liquidity preference and the money supply. If the transfer of income to a social group with a higher level of the marginal propensity to save does not change either the liquidity preference or the money supply ... , and if the marginal efficiency of capital is left unchanged, the increase in savings and consequent decrease in consumption will thus lead to a decrease in income, by reducing the effect of the investment multiplier.

> If savings were the key driver of investment, as most orthodox economists assume, income inequality would actually promote investment, by transferring income to those with a higher marginal propensity to save .... A central conclusion Keynes ... takes from his theory is that because this is not so, and because in the absence of full employment the key to economic recovery is the stimulation of aggregate demand, then his General Theory leads to a completely different social philosophy, where income equality is crucial to increase the investment multiplier and stimulate aggregate demand.[14]

It would appear from this prolix passage that inequality in an open and free market does not necessarily result in economic growth, or benefit economically developing states, since, as it happens, inequality reduces demand and the investment multiplier, which, by the way, intercepts the growth of their economy.

It is in the same spirit that rank Marxists rebuke neoliberalism for its inherent features, which are otherwise only characterized by the poverty that affects the lower classes. It is firmly believed that business owners (i.e., the bourgeoisie) seek more and more markets, through the forcible integration of emerging market economies into the global market, in order to increase the share of their large profits. For this purpose IFIs employ means of placing developing countries under the command of a single global market. In fact, it so chances, that, neo-colonialism (i.e., imperialism in a new disguise) has commenced new strategies, by which, as it seems, global governance undertakes to exploit workers, while extracting and conveying their wealth and resources from the periphery to the core countries—a notion which dependency theorists maintain. Now, this sort of enterprise is facilitated by the hegemonic leadership of the United States, whose soft-hard powers are invoked to direct and animate the pursuits of those emergent nations.

Unquestionably, India and most of the countries of modern Southeast Asia have been peculiarly successful in augmenting their pecuniary fortunes, contrary to what the IFIs have given nations to expect; and, as did eminently happen in the case of China, by dint of their protectionist policies (tax on imports, tariffs, etc.), they were capable of resisting the extensive ramifications of an economic crisis in 2008 long suspected to be approaching the European economy. On the other hand, those of their less distinguished neighbors of the Eurasian Steppe and the Caucasus who kept by the IMF's and the World Bank's recommendations, were attended with unhappy consequences. One example is found in Mongolia's liberalizing policies after the collapse of the Union of Soviet Socialist Republics (USSR), which imprudently wiped out the industrial sector that had been constructed in the last fifty years of the period of the Socialist state's incumbency.[15] If such a series of immediate results has any foundation in history, it probably relates to what is called "an initial period of infant-industry protection,"[16] which formerly opened the way to the proceedings of industrialization in the Global North, perhaps with the sole exception of the British Empire—it being the first industrialized empire that had not engaged at the time in the act of commercial competition with any rival. As it is, the different and various economic policies have caused a division betwixt emergent nations in proportion as they have adopted protectionist or liberalization policies; and so, upon the whole, Kiely assures us that economic growth does not arise from globalization.[17]

Of the other fruitless contracts of globalization, perhaps I ought to mention the intermittent flow of low investment capital from the Global North to the Global South. I have just the vacant space to give an illustration of this matter: firms do not transmit to the low-wage zones core activities which "depend on varied inputs, tacit knowledge, social contacts and closeness to consumers," but, on the contrary, heap their "labor-intensive parts of their value chains to low wage locations."[18] In point of minute accuracy, it may be recalled, "developing countries received 9.7% of global PI [portfolio investment] flows in 1991, 9.0% in 1994, 6.2% in 1998 and 5.5% in 2000."[19] This is also expressed in the knowledge, that "contrary to the common idea of markets and firms becoming increasingly global, most of the Fortune 500 biggest multinational corporations depend for most of their sales on their home region, whether North America, the European Union, or East Asia (the 'Triad')."[20] In sober judgment, this indicative conduct seems to intimate that international corporations do not possess an interest in the progress of the Global South, but prefer, thus conjured, the regionalizing expedients to the globalizing machinations.[21] The fact is, that "economic activities that are technological dead-ends, and thus only require unskilled labour, move to low-wage countries. Rich countries export products where there is great technological development and import products where there is little technological development."[22] And what is worst of all, should workers ever protest against their low wages, globalization would readily afford their employers the opportunity to withdraw their resources and relocate to another place in the low-wage zones.[23] With these reflections it may be supposed that developing countries cannot emulate their "northern" neighbors.

Author's Critique of Governance

As Hickey perceives, the new predilections for inquisitorial intervention and arithmetical supervision of emerging market economies, after the global financial crisis, seem consistent with the IFIs' express intention to secure the developing world's jacobitical loyalty to the compass of neoliberalism, regardless of any further loss or damages sustained by them.[24] In this manner, Third World countries are like birds entrapped in an ivy-tod, condemned to comply with the strict rules of free-trade agreements and requisite instructions singularly created for economies of an inferior rank, in order to appeal to the mercy of IFIs, in return for aid and loans of money.[25] IFIs not only demand liberalization and deregulation of the economy, but also require that underdeveloped countries procure structural alterations—changes that, in most cases, probably would be deleterious. If so, it has been insisted that, " 'normal' market processes—now fortified by WTO agreements that make many forms of industrial policy illegal—can therefore prevent firms and countries in the low wage zone from transforming themselves into attractive sites for higher quality work."[26] And we must presume that, because the Global South depends on imports from the Global North, it is somewhat deterred from domestic production.[27] In the meantime, finance is esteemed the "sector of choice" for predatory elites in IFIs,[28] who delight in the deliberate ignorance of the disastrous effects of Sorosian liberalization upon the political and social projections of those less developed countries at different points of the economic development spectrum.

Even now, though they pretend to stipulate for structural transformation, corrupt officials in the former colonies (such as the Republic of Indonesia) are chiefly entrusted by the IFIs with considerable sums of mercantile credit, and are not willing to support social development programs; partnerships and agreements are, therefore, more moved by deceitful rhetoric than by honest logic, and more attracted by selfish and unconscientious schemes of plundering their beneficiaries, than influenced by the merits of compassion upon the good of the Third World, consisting of about eighty-five per cent of the population in the varsal world.[29] In truth, it has been inferred, that any provision of welfare, such as primary healthcare, grants an easy method of sustaining a healthy workforce to maintain the productive labor required.[30] It is in the same spirit, if we are to judge from the more obviously evil purpose of minimal healthcare, that IFIs may abuse the deliberate system of education to indoctrinate the people in the same ideological—neoliberal—persuasion.[31] I am quite aware that the IMF seems, as a matter of course, to purchase research agendas encumbered by neoliberal tongues and neoliberal faces.[32]

In this particular, my eyes take the direction the counter-globalization movement points out; as it has been generally averred in internet manifestos and free-information websites, IFIs are hegemonized by Uncle Sam, to whose usual soft and hard powers must be added unaccountability, as well as a lack of transparency; so that the Global South, in the present circumstances, is likely underrepresented at the said institutions.[33] Concerning industrial policies, Wade tells us that the IFIs do not care to support the construction of industries in the developing world in order to replace "imports and challenge established ones in the West."[34] For Professor Cammack, it is the main object of the international financial institutions to accumulate capital and facilitate the proletarianization of the half-starved, half-clad citizens of the neo-colonies.[35] Thus the Gramscians conclude, "the institutions have been needlessly and incorrectly restricted to serve exclusively as agents of the ongoing hegemony and have thus been handicapped."[36]

Woodward admits, according to his computation of history, that the "current system of global economic governance itself dates back to the colonial era; and the decision-making structures established" (the IMF's weighted voting system, etc.) reflect the expectations of that era.[37] "The US government," Wade remarks, "was the primary architect of the international monetary system in place since the breakdown of the Bretton Woods system around 1970";[38] and, as one may expect, having the greater share of votes in the IMF and the World Bank, the United States can positively veto their proposed reforms or decisions, with a view to keeping guard over the obvious interests of the Land of Opportunity, whether they were to the prejudice of other states, or not.[39] Certainly, it is not surprising that agriculture in the United States is sheltered by the concealed manipulations of the IFIs. And further, the studied exercise of these powers combines with the cursed business of counting-houses, run by accountants intimately conversant with the books of accounts and money, transacted by that species of subjugated economies, to frustrate the efforts of counter-hegemonic social movements and political forces that at this time threaten the ascendancy of the Western world.[40] In any case, as the Global North finances these institutions, development programs in the Global South are not likely to prevail over their sponsors' affairs. To me, therefore, all these are signs that globalization, like the effect of a large tinfoil imperfectly flung over an old musty pie, has a villainous complexion masked by hypocrisy.

If such a tempting critique had any foundation in fact, it would probably relate to some statistical data on the reduction of poverty in consequence of globalization. Although in truth such a series of calculatory nets extracts a grain or two of the sense of pecuniary attainments arising behind, before, and around the First World, it neglects portraits of the internal features of global poverty, of which we may perhaps say that they implicate their (IFIs) reputation. In the first place, poverty quantified globally is far different from poverty quantified locally or between countries. It is important to remember this, because if newly industrialized countries (NICs), as the People's Republic of China, the Four Asian Tigers, and the Republic of India are called, are blotted out of the equations, it will soon appear that poverty rates have remained a long time unchanged amongst the rest of the NICs' followers. "Excluding China," as heard from the tenor of Woodward's voice, "the proportion of the world population living below the '$2-a-day' poverty line fell only from 49.7 percent in 1981 to 48.4 percent in 2005."[41]

Secondly, the quantitative methodologies designed to estimate the extent of the pretended abatement of poverty are distinctly illustrated in the choice betwixt the Penn World Tables for 1985 and the International Comparisons Project's 1993 Global Report, reported to the World Bank, in a manner the most favorable for the prospect of avowing the course of development in the extrication of global poverty beyond the period I have mentioned.[42] In these numerical epistles (it is said), there may be cause for disputatious deliberation, with much regard to the charge of the misprision of methodological treason; for though there is a sort of perspective in purchasing power parity (PPP), it is perfidious to take into account "all commodities, many of which are not consumed by the poor," rather than to follow a more suitable accentuation which would seek to identify consumed commodities only; meaning thereby to avoid the inclination to generalize consumption patterns.[43] A conjunction to this practice is that numbers do not give any account of the social problems they widely encounter. We need not refer to the rise of the gross domestic product (GDP) of low-income nations, and the almost proportionate decrease of poverty, the countenance of which, in most countries, cannot be relied upon.

The Concluding Death of Globalization

Having made an excursion for the discovery of the requisite lights upon the subject of global economic governance, the question now presents itself: As globalists pretend to cast the balance in favor of the wretched of the earth, should not they, as a rule, put down (suppress) their filial obedience to the *per contra*? On examination, we may conclude this account of globalization and its governance with the classic phrase, *pecunia non olet*. I have only to add that, both sides of the non-olfactory coin devote their active energies to the best advantage of that worshipful class of self-conceited depredators, with their "bloodless gums."[44] In such a state, as matters stand, the impropriety of excessive inequality still remains a dead letter. Kacowicz, alarmed at this easy conclusion, is determined that the fate of the globalist agenda shall depend on the extent and success of poverty relief.[45] It is also said, and truly, that the evidence brought against it makes a strong impression on my imagination,

> I, for one, somewhat startled, listened for the cry of Grendel, and the notes of Hygelac's horn and trumpets, and strained my eye on the operatic night sky, as if to descry the gold-laced dragon descending like a cloud of blood and flame, and disappearing. But, alas! all is silent, and Beowulf is no more to be dreaded as a slayer.

Such was the direction of my mind's eye, that when I set myself to consider the circumstances on which this narrative was founded, I turned to retrace the metaphorical steps of Mammon, and conceived it likely that one may throw the blame of vain promises upon the formidable bodies of monied interests that have marshalled globalization forward.

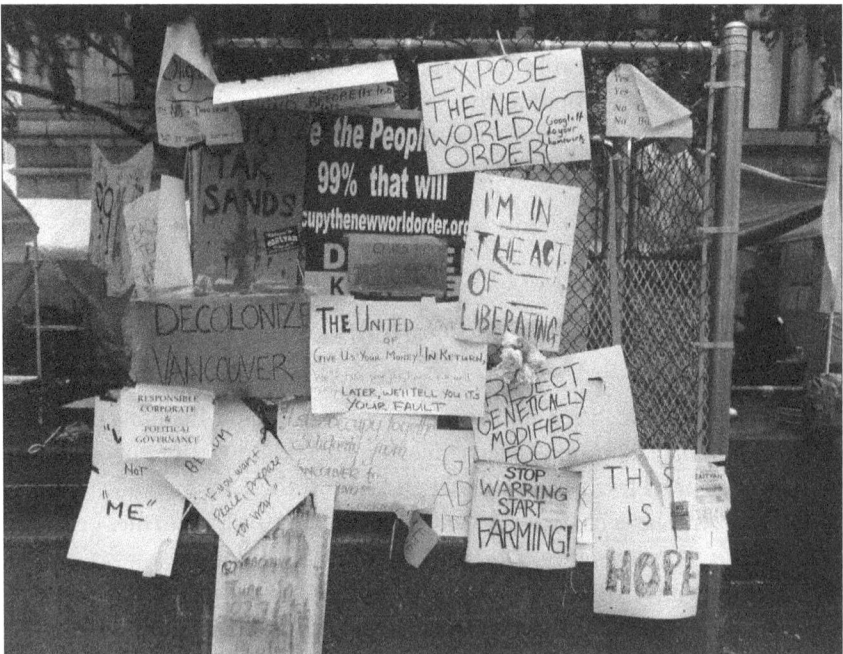

Figure 10.3. Various Occupy Vancouver signs attached to a fence.

Yet, in the fluctuations of equity, some may hope there is no ostensible ground for the calumny; for neoliberalists, as is well known, show "inequality provides incentives for effort and risk-taking, and thereby raises efficiency"; and, in the exaggeration of their good-will, they contend it is enough that the common people's condition is not made worse.[46] This point is very learnedly corrected by Wade, who professes that "this productive incentive effect applies only at moderate levels of inequality. At higher levels, such as in the USA over the past 20 years, it is likely to be swamped by social costs."[47] This, as I have already mentioned, and the sense of the obligations which IFIs owe to the indirect protection of their sponsors have turned globalization, unlike a commercial Hercules fit to sustain the weight of the sky, upside down. Even if, to all intents and purposes of investment, it is recollected that fortune has dawned upon some distinguished countries, as China and India, the nature of mutual aid and the constancy of attachment are far from consistent, as is seen in the rest of the developing world, which is so much lowered by the deprivations of their subjects; questionless, neither is it possible for us to doubt, that the gap in international inequality will be bridged in the meanwhile; and, judging from the progress they have made, they will probably remain comparatively marginalized in their asymmetric relationship.[48]

Postscript

To sum up my chapter (very shortly), globalization and its agents came under my critical inspection, by some discourse on the question of capital formation in historically marginalized developing countries. On perceiving the delicate nature of the debate in which I had engaged myself, my first idea was to attempt to speak on behalf of globalists. Specifically, I engaged in surveying the neoliberal tradition, the statistical account of globalization, and modernization theory. I then combated the arguments with some indignation; I had, as we have seen, particular recourse to the Marxian school of economics, and inferred that globalization, as an old and trusted agent of capitalism, is logically inconsistent; so that, no doubt, the institutions that initiate, by hook and by crook, those of a less advanced economy into the mysteries of "agio, tariffs, tare and tret"[49] have acquired the habit of sticking their carrot in front of yonder developing countries. Besides, I have heard from the military voice of Ben Brabyn, former Head of Level39 in Canary Wharf (whom I had occasion to curate as a speaker for my TEDxLambeth event in

2019 at the Royal Society for the Encouragement of Arts, Manufactures and Commerce), that "trickle-down economics isn't working anymore."[50] But, seriously—well judging that there is justice (to all mankind) for wrong either in heaven or on earth, globalists will do well to beware how they might ensure a correspondence between their actions and their future karma prospects.

As an aside, the original manuscript ends here somewhat abruptly, as if fearful of saying too much. John Barnwell and Leo Lyon Zagami have intelligence enough in a secret drawer of their oaken escritoire to think that what follows relates chiefly to some plan of a One World Order!

ENDNOTES

[1]   Ray Kiely, "Globalization and Poverty, and the Poverty of Globalization Theory," *Current Sociology* 53, no. 6 (2005): 896, https://doi.org/10.1177/0011392105057154.

[2]   David William Parry, "Gemini City," in *Voices of Friends Poetry and Art Almanac 2024*, ed. John Farndon, Marina Podlesnaya, and David William Parry ([Hemel Hempstead, UK?]: Hertfordshire Press, 2023), 23.

[3]   Arie M. Kacowicz, "Globalization, Poverty, and the North-South Divide," *International Studies Review* 9, no. 4 (December 2007): 573, https://doi.org/10.1111/j.1468-2486.2007.00723.x.

[4]   Lloyd Gruber, "Globalisation with Growth and Equity: Can We Really Have It All?," *Third World Quarterly* 32, no. 4 (2011): 632, https://www.jstor.org/stable/41300339; Robert Hunter Wade, "On the Causes of Increasing World Poverty and Inequality, or Why the Matthew Effect Prevails," *New Political Economy* 9, no. 2 (2004): 164, https://doi.org/10.1080/1356346042000218050; Lindsay Whitfield, "How Countries Become Rich and Reduce Poverty: A Review of Heterodox Explanations of Economic Development," *Development Policy Review* 30, no. 3 (May 2012): 239–260, https://doi.org/10.1111/j.1467-7679.2012.00575.x.

[5]   Kacowicz, "Globalization, Poverty, and the North-South Divide," 571.

[6]   Wade, "On the Causes of Increasing World Poverty and Inequality, or Why the Matthew Effect Prevails," 164.

[7]   "Poverty Overview," World Bank, last updated October 7, 2014, https://web.archive.org/web/20150214050250/https://www.worldbank.org/en/topic/poverty/overview.

[8]   Wade, "On the Causes of Increasing World Poverty and Inequality, or Why the Matthew Effect Prevails," 169.

[9]   Whitfield, "How Countries Become Rich and Reduce Poverty," 239ff.

[10]   Joshua Cooper Ramo, "The Three Marketeers," *Time*, February 15, 1999, https://time.com/archive/6955233/the-three-marketeers-2/.

[11]   Sam Hickey, "Beyond 'Poverty Reduction Through Good Governance': The New Political Economy of Development in Africa," *New Political Economy* 17, no. 5 (2012): 685ff., https://doi.org/10.1080/13563467.2012.732274.

[12]   Nuno Martins, "Globalisation, Inequality and the Economic Crisis," *New Political Economy* 16, no. 1 (2011): 8, https://doi.org/10.1080/13563461003789761.

[13]   Gruber, "Globalisation with Growth and Equity," 634.

[14]   Martins, "Globalisation, Inequality and the Economic Crisis," 7–8.

[15]   Wade, "On the Causes of Increasing World Poverty and Inequality, or Why the Matthew Effect Prevails," 181.

[16]   Whitfield, "How Countries Become Rich and Reduce Poverty," 249.

[17]   Kiely, "Globalization and Poverty, and the Poverty of Globalization Theory," 895ff.

[18]   Wade, "On the Causes of Increasing World Poverty and Inequality, or Why the Matthew Effect Prevails," 173–174.

[19]   Ilene Grabel, "International Private Capital Flows and Developing Countries," in *Rethinking Development Economics*, ed. Ha-Joon Chang (London: Anthem Press, 2003), 327.

[20]   Wade, "On the Causes of Increasing World Poverty and Inequality, or Why the Matthew Effect Prevails," 175.

[21]   Wade, "On the Causes of Increasing World Poverty and Inequality, or Why the Matthew Effect Prevails," 177.

[22]   Whitfield, "How Countries Become Rich and Reduce Poverty," 249.

[23]   Gruber, "Globalisation with Growth and Equity," 639.

[24]   Hickey, "Beyond 'Poverty Reduction Through Good Governance,' " 684ff.

[25]   Julie L. Mueller, "The IMF, Neoliberalism and Hegemony," *Global Society* 25, no. 3 (2011): 390, https://doi.org/10.1080/13600826.2011.577032; Hickey, "Beyond 'Poverty Reduction Through Good Governance,' " 684–685.

[26]   Wade, "On the Causes of Increasing World Poverty and Inequality, or Why the Matthew Effect Prevails," 173.

[27]   Wade, "On the Causes of Increasing World Poverty and Inequality, or Why the Matthew Effect Prevails," 175.

[28]   Wade, "On the Causes of Increasing World Poverty and Inequality, or Why the Matthew Effect Prevails," 178.

[29]   David Woodward, "Democratizing Global Governance for Sustainable Human Development," *Development* 53, no. 1 (2010): 42, https://doi.org/10.1057/dev.2009.85.

[30]   Paul Cammack, "What the World Bank Means by Poverty Reduction, and Why It Matters," *New Political Economy* 9, no. 2 (June 2004): 191, 199, https://doi.org/10.1080/1356346042000218069.

[31]   Cammack, "What the World Bank Means by Poverty Reduction, and Why It Matters," 202; Mueller, "The IMF, Neoliberalism and Hegemony," 384, 387, 391.

[32]   Mueller, "The IMF, Neoliberalism and Hegemony," 391.

[33]   Mark Engler, "Defining the Anti-Globalization Movement," *Democracy Uprising*, April 1, 2007, https://democracyuprising.com/2007/04/01/anti-globalization-movement/.

[34]   Wade, "On the Causes of Increasing World Poverty and Inequality, or Why the Matthew Effect Prevails," 181.

[35]   Cammack, "What the World Bank Means by Poverty Reduction, and Why It Matters," 190.

[36]   Frederick H. Gareau, "International Institutions and the Gramscian Legacy: Its Modification, Expansion, and Reaffirmation," *The Social Science Journal* 33, no. 2 (1996): 224, https://doi.org/10.1016/S0362-3319(96)90038-5.

[37]   Woodward, "Democratizing Global Governance for Sustainable Human Development," 43.

[38]   Wade, "On the Causes of Increasing World Poverty and Inequality, or Why the Matthew Effect Prevails," 179.

[39]   Woodward, "Democratizing Global Governance for Sustainable Human Development," 43.

[40]   Gareau, "International Institutions and the Gramscian Legacy," 226.

[41]   Woodward, "Democratizing Global Governance for Sustainable Human Development," 43.

[42]   Kiely, "Globalization and Poverty, and the Poverty of Globalization Theory," 896.

[43]   Kiely, "Globalization and Poverty, and the Poverty of Globalization Theory," 897.

[44]   David William Parry, unpublished manuscript.

[45]   Kacowicz, "Globalization, Poverty, and the North-South Divide," 571.

[46]   Wade, "On the Causes of Increasing World Poverty and Inequality, or Why the Matthew Effect Prevails," 182.

[47]   Wade, "On the Causes of Increasing World Poverty and Inequality, or Why the Matthew Effect Prevails," 182.

[48]   Kacowicz, "Globalization, Poverty, and the North-South Divide," 571.

[49]   Sir Walter Scott, *Rob Roy, Complete, Illustrated* (Boston, 1893; Project Gutenberg, 2018), https://www.gutenberg.org/files/7025/7025-h/7025-h.htm.

[50]   Ben Brabyn, "Ambition and Humility: Reconnecting Business with Community," filmed October 2019 in London, UK, TEDx video, https://youtu.be/cd1zXVY8EUw?si=Z3qS2L7fsVrXTDHW. Other speakers in this gathering included the Rev. David William Parry, Haralampi G. Oroschakoff, and Prof. Andy Clark.

CHAPTER XI

DISCOURSES OF TRUTH:
A NOTE ON POWER RELATIONS AND POWER STRUCTURES

There is comprised, in one debate concerning the question between the delivery and perception of truth, and the sort and degree of power, the chronological field of political theory and the philosophy of sociology: and they that have been reading the French philosopher Paul-Michel Foucault will be still more likely to apply utility to his structural histories, his knowledge, his power, and so forth. In Philip Stokes's *Philosophy: 100 Essential Thinkers*, "The theme," it is said, "that underlies all Foucault's work is the relationship between power and knowledge, and how the former is used to control and define the latter."[1] It may be, Foucault says, "that truth isn't outside power or lacking in power, . . . truth isn't the reward of free spirits, the child of protracted solitude, nor the privilege of those who have succeeded in liberating themselves. Truth is a thing of this world: it is produced only by virtue of multiple forms of constraint. And it induces regular effects of power."[2] Be it so—for the purpose of the present inquiry, be it so; but, if so it be, let the explanation of the discourses of truth and their respective inscriptions beneath the superstructure of power be received. On this occasion, to the feline eyes of that same purring homosexual more particularly, who is a perfect master of serious consideration of any intervening truth (knowledge in the broad sense of the word) in the exercise of power (as will be seen), must our panopticon gaze be directed. All this while, the subject in question has been interpreted by the instructive operations of the academic and the scholar whom I will come to speak of in order to have the clearer view of the grounds of the narrative.

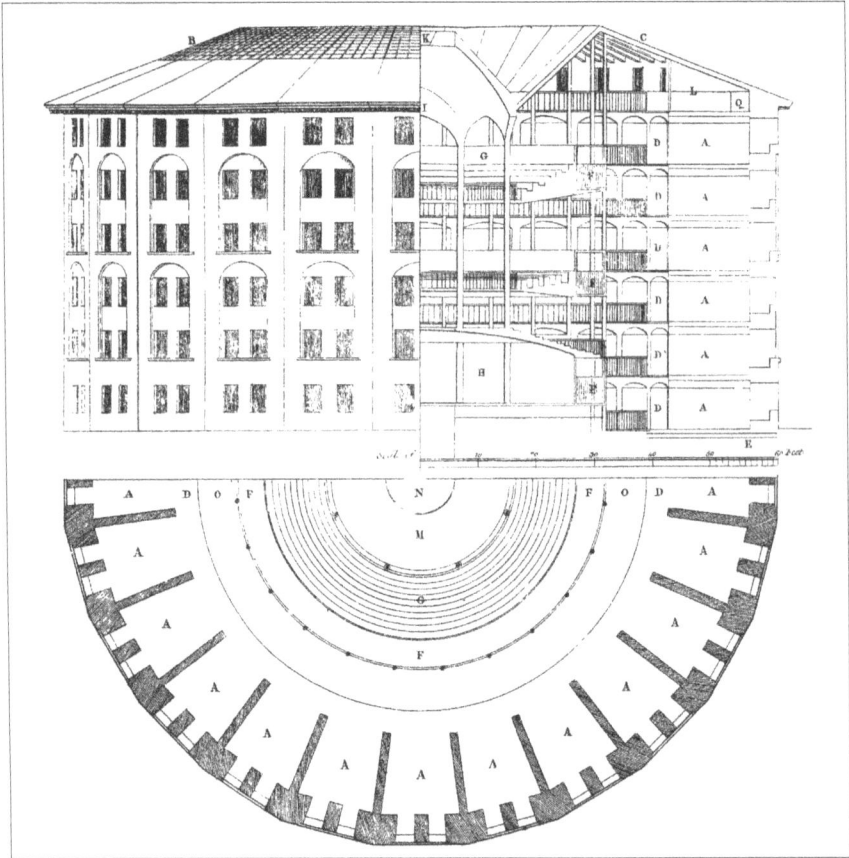

Figure 11.1. Plan of the panopticon by Jeremy Bentham.

In this eleventh chapter, I hope to engage the reader's attention, and present to his—or to one of any alternate-gendered person's—avidity a clear view of the terms employed, to wit, the superstructure of power and the words of truth, in speaking of the arguments, suited to the question, so as to cover the whole complexion of the standard narrative, meaning the definition, at the hands of the professor of the history of systems of thought, Doctor Foucault. Then I undertake to ascertain the specific arrangements, and to draw inferences from them. Follows thereupon a summary view, accompanied by an answer to the question why are discourses of truth inscribed in power relations and power structures. For this purpose, the chapter may be considered as divided into four sections, like those of the other chapters, a mere instrument of academic communication. Whatsoever may be the force of these narratives, little weight will here be attached to any assertion, for reasons which I have left you to guess, and this, after a voyage of some length in this epistle of mine. Neither ought I to give an explicit analysis of the Frenchman's claims concerning anything beyond the making of this long-studied text, though implicitly, the idea of such a connection, to wit, between power and truth, has been conveyed in that author's earlier writings, to wit, *Madness and Civilization: A History of Insanity in the Age of Reason* and *The Birth of the Clinic: An Archaeology of Medical Perception*, etc.

Not Truth, But Power

Foucault's own account of the matter is in its complexion truly worthy here of notice, to be understood in a manner other than that of some unjust a priori reasoning. As such do I seek to have a clearer view of the origin, as well as the particular meaning, of the words of the philosopher: and this part might, not altogether without ground, help to give additional credence to the purpose of our argument at least.

Accordingly, the idea conveyed by the word *discourse* may perhaps be the most important point of perfect information. Of the discourse in question, Iara Lessa defined it in terms of "systems of thoughts composed of ideas, attitudes, courses of action, beliefs and practices that systematically construct the subjects and the worlds of which they speak."[3] Foucault himself wrote at one time in his book, *The Archaeology of Knowledge*, that it could be interpreted as a "way of speaking."[4] In the meantime, Clare O'Farrell regarded it as the material "verbal traces left behind by history."[5] Truly, then, innumerable are the functions in which the word *discourse* may be found to have its use, which, if reported as diffusing knowledge and "truth," would here be relevant for the purposes of the present question.[6] In the hope of augmenting the color of truth, it will be noticed that "certain discourses in certain contexts have the power to convince people to accept statements as true."[7] In this observation, it is believed, "The medical practice of leeching was accepted in the eighteenth century as helpful despite the harmful affects that we recognize today because it was embedded in a network of ancient medical discourses" which were generally received as conclusive:[8] in the same breath, Dr Clayton J. Whisnant said, "Many medical practices commonly accepted today might have seemed like madness or even barbaric because they had no discursive support."[9] But, in the case of discourse and power, it may be observed, that "discourse operates, namely by being intimately involved with socially embedded networks of power."[10] Some persons, namely those who are known to be experts in certain questions, shall thereby be the better enabled to "speak the truth" or, at least, "to be believed when speaking on specific subjects," and in that case give them "degrees of social, cultural, and even possibly political power":[11] for example, belief in the work of the doctor, under and by the authority of whom the illness of the physical or mental frame is to be believed, and which, supposing them believed, "gives them an authority to recommend courses of action or patterns of behavior" in a society.[12] What is more, in the same manner and on the same principles, the religious constituted authorities, however sublimely, "wielded tremendous social and political power because they had the power to speak about the divine."[13] By some people, all this discourse of truth will of course seem to refer to a simplicity of conception and ideation in various and mutually distant contexts.

The Looking Glass

Further on, materially different is the power supposed to have been exercised by the direction of existing institutions, or accredited and credited agents, from that of any of the Foucauldian accounts: and that because of the special approach made, distinct from the main one; "power is not essentially something that institutions possess and use oppressively against individuals and groups":[14] power, for the purpose mentioned, "is more like something that acts and operates in a certain way," in which it is "more a strategy than a possession."[15] Here, power, it may be affirmed without impropriety, is "co-extensive with resistance, as a productive factor, because it has positive effects such as the individual's self-making, and because, as a condition of possibility for any relation, it is ubiquitous, being found in any type of relation between the members of society."[16] In this trance, power would absolutely be "the relations between the individual and the society, especially its institutions."[17] But at the same time, Foucault sought to divert the advocacy of his principles of government from the Marxian persuasion, which takes for granted that the powerless, by the powerful, are subjected, under their institutions.[18] On the contrary, we see, "power relations dissipate through all relational structures of the society."[19] For, what is expressly stated, "I am not referring to Power—with a capital P—dominating and imposing its rationality upon the totality of the social body. In fact, there are power relations. They are multiple; they have different forms, they can be in play in family relations, or within an institution, or an administration."[20] Foucault contended that power, if anything, "must be analysed as something which circulates, or rather as something which only functions in the form of a chain. . . . Power is employed and exercised through a net-like organization. . . . Individuals are the vehicles of power, not its points of application."[21]

A Fragment

To a second glance the omnipresence of power "can be found in all social interactions," no matter how "intimate and egalitarian" the interactions are to be carried on.[22] To this, he, in his narrative, at the time in question, of the matter in question, in the instance in question, added, "It seems to me that power *is* 'always already there,' " (italics in the original) whereas, "one is never 'outside' it."[23] Yet, even this is not all: for, "Without resistance, without two bodies (or minds) pushing or pulling against each other, there is no power relation."[24] After all, what is not said is—knowledge that is but "recognized as true," and "known to be the case," is decreed or proffered by an authoritative hand "from on high," but, on the contrary, is more particularly "described in the passive voice," in so far as it "can only exist with the support of arrangements of power, arrangements that likewise have no clear origin, no person or body," that may be found to "have" it.[25] As to the general and formal denomination of state power,—"the state is not mainly something that owns power, but rather something which builds a system of relations between individuals so that the political system works."[26] Of the contrast between power and power, it is written and concluded that "power was exerted in various stages of European history and shows how the monarchic power system was replaced by the democratic one."[27] So that, in the original, accounts given of any such monarchical power, in the supposed accounts of all these supposed punitive imaginable means, is of course represented by the intensity of public sacrifices. Executions? Yes, that they did; but "that of democratic power is discipline, imprisonment away from public eyes."[28] In this particular, considering the disciplinary instrument of their self-regulation, by which the behavior and reality of an individual might be affected, no censorship, no abstraction, no exclusion, no repression, no masks, no concealment, are compelled by it: from the manner in which power is mentioned, the most express negative terms seem improbable; if so, "power produces; it produces reality; it produces domains of objects and rituals of truth."[29] In a word, "relations of power, and hence the analysis that must be made of them, necessarily extend beyond the limits of the state."[30] The first appropriate and sufficient reason is—that "the state, for all the omnipotence of its apparatuses, is far from being able to occupy the whole field of actual power relations; and, further, because the state can only operate on the basis of other, already-existing power relations."[31]

A Dialogue

On the supposition of the influence of discipline, speaking of this all-important "strategy," the case seems to be—that, the relations of power contained in history style the "truth" as belonging to individuals. This is natural enough. In part, "through certain *spatial* disposition of individuals" (italics in the original): namely, in prisons, hospitals, schools, army barracks, psychiatric clinics,—individuals may be perceived as segregated into heterogeneous groups, like so many of soldiers and officers who live in separate rooms so as to continue all pretensions of hierarchical control.[32] They therefore, being given treatment on unequal terms, come to "know their place," which, "in the context of the general economy of space," connects with any such disciplinary power.[33] True it is, that, Mr. Bentham's own expectation was, the panopticon would serve as an allusion to a laboratory that "could be used as a machine to carry out experiments, to alter behavior, to train or correct individuals."[34] Take the example of the experience of Nathan at the age of 4; teased by his fellow classmates, because he enjoyed playing "like a girl."[35] Employed in the endeavor at the extremities, indeed, of this "productive network of power which runs through the whole social body," the exposure of Nathan's violation of the ordinary course of things is instrumental in one or another of two ways: in this instance alone, "it rouses the apparatus that will therapeutically draft Nathan into his prescribed role and correct the parental missteps that resulted in Nathan's deviation; it also provides an opportunity to produce new knowledge," or, to take the choice of other eulogistic words, new "understandings," new "truths," not only in relation to Nathan, but likewise in regard to the children and parents in this increasing world "who would be identified under this new disorder."[36] In this observation may be seen an example of the scientific ingredients in the authoritative composition of "truth."

Lastly there comes a brief preparatory indication of the effect of discontinuity in the study of science, steadfastly beholding that any such thing

> is not a change of content (refutation of old errors, recovery of old truths), nor is it a change of theoretical form (renewal of a paradigm, modification of systematic ensembles). It is a question of what *governs* statements, and the way in which they *govern* [italics in the original] each other so as to constitute a set of propositions that are scientifically acceptable and, hence, capable of being verified or falsified by scientific procedures. In short, there is a problem of the regime, the politics of the scientific statement.[37]

In a case of this sort, then, the frequent emergence of new theories of science very much depends upon the superstructure of power, rather than discussion and correlation: the conveyance of which may determine the order in which they are enumerated.

Conclusion: The Supposable Arguments Summed Up

In this chapter, under the title of "Discourses of Truth: A Note on Power Relations and Power Structures," my expectation was to find some explanation of the inscription of the discourses of truth in power relations and power structures, in the reading of that vision which everybody looks for from Foucault. I verily thought that power may be seen—seen in positive terms, instead of its being negatively related, as to be productive of the consequence, the practical consequence. For, power relations, whose nature is everywhere, will be still more likely to experience strenuous resistance. As to the consequence of it, we would see the necessity of the comparative significance of the process, as in the case of new discourses of truth and knowledge. That the indissoluble bond of connection between, and channel of intercourse interwoven so especially in the texture of, the state of science and the state itself on the one hand, and power, or truth, on the other hand, is sufficiently established, cannot be denied. Bearing all this in mind, let me say plainly and simply, it seems reasonable to conclude, that the evidence is good in support of Foucault's visions.

ENDNOTES

[1] Philip Stokes, *Philosophy: 100 Essential Thinkers: The Ideas That Have Shaped Our World* (London: Arcturus Publishing, 2012), 342.

[2] Michel Foucault, *Power*, ed. James D. Faubion, trans. Hobert Hurley and others (New York: New Press, 2000), 131.

[3] Iara Lessa, "Discursive Struggles Within Social Welfare: Restaging Teen Motherhood," *British Journal of Social Work* 36, no. 2 (2006): 285, https://www.jstor.org/stable/23720912.

[4] Michel Foucault, *The Archaeology of Knowledge and the Discourse on Language*, trans. A. M. Sheridan Smith (London: Tavistock Publications, 1972), 193.

[5] Clare O'Farrell, *Michel Foucault* (London: Sage Publications, 2005), 78.

[6] Clayton Whisnant, "Foucault & Discourse: A Handout for HIS 389," last modified November 9, 2012, https://web.archive.org/web/20120208013606/http://webs.wofford.edu/whisnantcj/his389/foucault_discourse.pdf.

[7] Whisnant, "Foucault & Discourse."

[8] Whisnant, "Foucault & Discourse."

[9] Whisnant, "Foucault & Discourse."

[10] Whisnant, "Foucault & Discourse."

[11] Whisnant, "Foucault & Discourse."

[12] Whisnant, "Foucault & Discourse."

[13] Whisnant, "Foucault & Discourse."

[14] Sergiu Bălan, "M. Foucault's View on Power Relations," *Cogito—Multidisciplinary Research Journal* 2, no. 2 (2010): 55.

[15] Bălan, "M. Foucault's View on Power Relations," 55.

[16] Bălan, "M. Foucault's View on Power Relations," 55.

[17] Bălan, "M. Foucault's View on Power Relations," 55.

[18] Bălan, "M. Foucault's View on Power Relations," 56.

[19] Bălan, "M. Foucault's View on Power Relations," 56.

[20] Michel Foucault, *Politics, Philosophy, Culture: Interviews and Other Writings 1977–1984*, ed. Lawrence D. Kritzman, trans. Alan Sheridan and Others (London: Routledge, 1988), 38.

[21] Michel Foucault, *Power/Knowledge: Selected Interviews and Other Writings 1972–1977*, ed. Colin Gordon, trans. Colin Gordon and Others (New York: Pantheon Books, 1980), 98.

22   Richard A. Lynch, "Foucault's Theory of Power," in *Michel Foucault: Key Concepts*, ed. Dianna Taylor (Durham, UK: Acumen, 2011), 15.

23   Foucault, *Power/Knowledge*, 141.

24   Lynch, "Foucault's Theory of Power," 24.

25   Ellen K. Feder, "Power/Knowledge," in *Michel Foucault: Key Concepts*, ed. Dianna Taylor (Durham, UK: Acumen, 2011), 56.

26   Bălan, "M. Foucault's View on Power Relations," 58.

27   Bălan, "M. Foucault's View on Power Relations," 58.

28   Bălan, "M. Foucault's View on Power Relations," 58.

29   Michel Foucault, *Discipline and Punish: The Birth of the Prison*, 2nd ed., trans. Alan Sheridan (New York: Vintage Books, 1995), 194.

30   Foucault, *Power*, 122–123.

31   Foucault, *Power*, 123.

32   Bălan, "M. Foucault's View on Power Relations," 59.

33   Bălan, "M. Foucault's View on Power Relations," 59.

34   Foucault, *Discipline and Punish*, 203.

35   Feder, "Power/Knowledge," 57.

36   Feder, "Power/Knowledge," 60.

37   Foucault, *Power*, 114.

PART IV

GLOBAL FACTIONS

CHAPTER XII

AN EXTEMPORE EFFUSION ON THE SUPERIORITY OF FICTION OVER NONFICTION

> Traditionally, critics cite fictionality as the most common feature distinguishing a novel from historical composition: a perfect specimen being narrative set in the future, like Ethan of Athos, an English language science fiction novel by American author Lois McMaster Bujold (born 1949).
>
> —David William Parry, *Mount Athos Inside Me*

I was asked once to prepare a seminar on the superiority of reading literature over academic texts around the subject area of postcolonialism. Of course, postcolonialism is a particular field of study concerned with the impact of former (European) colonizers on the so-called colonized; sometimes referred to nowadays as the developing, or third world, nations. In which case, no doubt, as an Anglo-Iranian-Romanian in Scotland, this subject matter resonated within me deeply; especially considering the sensitive divide between foreigner and native, as well as my own social status as an immigrant.

As it happened, the seminar received positive reviews, even though, ironically, I was not eager to agree with my own "conclusions." Indeed, I felt my judgment was overly shaped by implicit pressures from an academic environment in which the seminar had been completed. In this regard, I should mention I particularly felt urged, if not actually coerced, by the expectant dispositions embedded inside current academia: namely, the predominant influence of scientific frameworks built upon reason, logic and clear-cut analyses—frameworks which in most instances result in ideologically "balanced" conclusions. Accordingly, I was compelled to veer away from clearly anticipatory judgments supported by censure. In other words, I felt independent insights might not be received well in academia, which is why I followed the usual road taken at that time.

Therefore, my present overview breathes new breath. Personally, I fervently believe in the superiority of literature over academic compositions. My decision, to be sure, is individually attested through a very simple intuition. At the end of the day, it is literature that gifts us with a far deeper "understanding" of postcolonial issues, solutions, and a sense of historical witness—a stance thereby providing effectual growth and development within our transnational collective consciousness.

Impromptu

Essentially, works of fiction transfer sophisticated knowledge, along with an obviously penetrative understanding, in the form of symbols, metaphors, emotions and experiences, which are accessible to the reading public far more readily than any analysis within academic essaying. The general public, after all, is not normally required to train (in the same vein as academics) in rigorous analyses of highly complex information.

So stated, although relevant works of fiction are certainly not few in number, one must be careful in one's preferences: particularly in light of the possible assumption that all works of fiction are equal in intellectual and emotional worth. In this sense, *Harry Potter* of J. K. Rowling, the "vampires" and "werewolves" of Stephenie Meyer, or the *Fifty Grey, Darker and Freed Shades* of E. L. James simply do not evolve our grasp of the world, even if they are considered page-turners.

The Vision

Rather, if I dare say so, we should try to focus on the other, often neglected, end of literature; a sphere frequently referred to as literary fiction, or, perhaps more appropriately, conceptually based literature. For example, *Shooting an Elephant* by George Orwell, *A Passage to India* by E. M. Forster, *Anita and Me* by Meera Syal or, for that matter, *Fight Club* by Chuck Palahniuk are all worthy (and celebrated) works of fiction that relate in one way, or another, to postcolonial trajectories within our current "international" culture.

Beyond doubt, one instance that does this particularly well is Chinua Achebe's *Things Fall Apart*, with its singularly rich description of pre- and intra-colonial Nigeria—its elaborate indigenous culture, religion, food, music, dance and other exotic traditions. Furthermore, Achebe's bold and demanding characters are nothing less than relatable. Therefore, we, as readers, seem to "naturally" empathize with their emotions, experiences and inmost thoughts. In this sense, their successes and failures become our own in the subjective community we simultaneously inhabit. Moreover, perceived relationships betwixt Nigerian husbands and wives, fathers and sons, mothers and daughters, and so forth, echo with this wider audience. In an almost mystical sense,

> We have all become "One"—we have all become "One"—we have all become "One" within shared experiences.

Truly, by tapping into our imagination, not to mention immersing ourselves in a variety of creative scenarios and narratives, one is enduringly made aware of ideas previously unknown that, by and large, are hidden by the turmoil of day-to-day routines of life. It is a "soul-making" journey, one may say, guiding and leading us all to places uncharted within ourselves. What is more, each reader is enthused to act and engender change—our thoughts and actions subtly altered—for we have now climbed inside one another's skin; paraphrasing Atticus in *To Kill a Mockingbird*.

A Conclusion Added in a Mason Lodge

On that note, one might add a remarkable fact about Schopenhauer, in that he (as an unarguably adept philosopher himself) placed art above philosophy. Obviously, this leads somehow to the inference that it is not just serious literature which can enlighten our minds, but equally "serious" music, theater, poetry and painting. Undoubtedly, there should be no hesitancy in claims corroborating that the world of entertainment and popular culture has their place in our lives: including shameless productions like *The Lion King* and *Matilda* on West End and Broadway stages.

Yet, in our present condition of uncertainty, doubt and distrust, what we really need is a deeper existential understanding tutored by, above all, compassion towards our fellow human beings wherever they may be from. So, my contention is that serious works of a free imagination delve into our shared predicament more effectively than graphs, or surveys. Certainly, as an immigrant myself, these were the types of material which truly explained and contextualized my own circumstances when I arrived as a "stranger in a strange land."

Epilogue

This, no doubt, was the approach I took in my previous books. I studiously undertook, in a sense, with my historical imagination, to be the hero of my own tale.

CHAPTER XIII

REFLECTIONS AND REMARKS ON POSTCOLONIAL QUESTIONS: A PROPOSAL TO EMBRACE LITERARY NOVELS AND ACADEMIC TEXTS

The greatest part of prose writings of our modern times may be divided into two classes: that of academic texts, which fall short of the heights of popularity; and that of novels and romances of the highest caliber, which rise beyond the natural bent of the mind. The latter class are by far the most uncommon; and, to which I may add, by far the most useful and valuable. When I deliberated, in 2016, concerning this variety of fine compositions, I was then a student at the University of Wales, Aberystwyth, under the same roof as Professor Jenny Edkins, and not quite free from the alloy of the agreement and convention among those in the speculative positivist sciences, and passed my time in the expectations of a balance of argument, drawn more from views of detached objectivity than from subjectivity.

But to observe the illicit submission with which the many resign their own minds to those of their instructors, or tutors, is very tempting to the mode of analytic philosophy, so agreeable in Anglophone countries; which, in my own opinion, is not so certain as is pretended. This (originally Gramscian) page begins several pages of my commentaries more from the manner than the matter of my eyes over the whole face of literary monographs. Every judgment and conclusion, with me, therefore, is not popular, but is founded on previously made advances in academies and literary masterpieces that I had consumed at university. I was, I confess, encouraged in this affair by the example of Philip K. Dick's *Valis* given to me by the Valentinian Gnostic Tau, D. W. Parry.

Figure 13.1. Philip K. Dick, in 1962 or earlier; films based on his stories include *Blade Runner* (1982), *Total Recall* (1990), *Minority Report* (2002), and *A Scanner Darkly* (2006).

Of Things Falling Apart

Here, then, is a sufficient inducement to consider the matter in its proper light, and that we shall examine only one novel, *Things Fall Apart* (1958) by Chinua Achebe, a concise writer, and select writings of postcolonial theorists. I will venture to assert that both these textual compositions are of peculiar and natural advantages and disadvantages, and that the public would be much more prudent were they to make use of these departments of knowledge. I maintain that novels can augment the meaning of postcolonial questions and enforce the execution of decolonization which now prevails; whereas academic writings provide a system of directions for the understanding of postcolonial issues and decoloniality by a sensible current that shall endeavor to open the eyes of the public. To which we may add that throughout this discourse, the idea of the subaltern (or, in other words, the lower sort of people, who are cruelly oppressed by a few masters) is situated near the center of my seminar.

I think an introduction to the story of Okonkwo, the central character of *Things Fall Apart*, and the theme of the novel, is necessary before the following reflections. It is well known that Albert Chinụalụmọgụ Achebe, in his first novel, aimed only at the possibility of giving a voice to Africa.[1] Having read the literature of the English language, he had taken notice of "a gap in the bookshelf" that needed to be filled with the books of indigenous writers,[2] not the industry of the white of all European nations; and, in the meanwhile, if we consult history, this practice of European colonizers—of encumbering their colonies with a thin veil of mystery of the philosophy of the "experts"—was also recognized by Professor Edward Wadie Said.[3] The former was a man of great sense and courage, whose chief writings were his account of the state of society that prevailed in the pre-colonial era, and the ill effects arising from poisoned interests, factions, corruptions, and disorders, incidental to the tyranny of their colonizers.

The protagonist, Okonkwo, lives in Umuofia, a fictional village in the southern part of Nigeria. He is not only a wealthy and respected man, who has married three wives and propagated young children, but has also acted all along with the dignity of a leader in his community—and he has become a kind of leader in the village, in consequence of the sentiments of envy he harbored towards masculinity, which was esteemed an evident sign of the strength of any person. The narrator in this narration gives us the detail of the particulars: Okonkwo's father, despised for his effeminacy, weakness, and hated for his poverty, had no hopes of making any progress that could discharge his debts before the death of the preceding generation. In twenty-five chapters, the whole tenor of the narrator is called upon to give a detailed description of the thoughts of our warrior and other imaginary characters of the story, by every captious rule of logic, as well as the old system of manners and customs of the inhabitants of Nigeria, such as the mutilation of their infants who had perished from bodily sickness, called *iba*, the worship of woods and stones as minor gods, and the practice of leaving twin infants in the Evil Forest, in the pre-colonial period. One would imagine that the life and actions of a villager would prove disagreeable to the moral reasonings of all European minds. In the second part, we learn from Achebe that the first step after the establishment of the European yoke was the introduction of gradual changes in their ways of living, so that the whole tribe fell apart. In the last part of *Things Fall Apart* as Okonkwo is not able to resist these concessions in his own village community, he has resolution enough to commit suicide, signalizing in this manner his people's demise precipitately.

That Novels May Be Better

We return now to the foregoing question of whether in reality novels are better than academic writings so far as they regard postcolonialism. If we reflect on this, we shall be apt to think of a person who has not reasoned on this subject, or, if you will, the refined ideas of hegemony, essentialism, colonial discourse, othering, subalternity, and so on. In this respect, let us imagine that this person is as much inferior to others in power as in knowledge, and, in the meanwhile, they are buried in profound ignorance. I may now ask whether novels may be more favorable to emancipation than academic writings. Thus, they might approach and enter more deeply into the subject of postcolonialism, with a pen and paper (and coffee!). Being unaccustomed to a more plentiful way of life, they can read Achebe's *Things Fall Apart* and may draw parallels from the received themes in his narration, which is so much illustrated by the example of *chi*, or destiny, and whether it should fall under the arms of the individuals. What the reader would readily perceive from the same origin, to be sure, may perhaps to some appear hard to conceive, though Okonkwo's passions of masculinity, ambition, and fortune, are obvious instances to the same purpose. Yet, even with this allowance, it must be allowed that, since the same person engaged in that labor may easily be diverted from the improvements of their disadvantages to the relish of selfishness, inattention to others, and indolence, while their subalternity is entirely overlooked and neglected. To be sure, such a perpetual scene of stagnation is supplied by the conception of "the Privileges of Amnesia," as articulated by Sankaran Krishna.[4]

Were it otherwise the method of reading the relevant academic writings would give directions for the same reason above mentioned, and would tell them what to look for. Besides, the academic text provides an in-depth analysis of the chief pillars of their postcolonial theory, its constituent parts, and serves to give an unaffected description of the doctrines above mentioned. What possible advantage is there that the reader can reap by the perusal of some novels? I answer, if novels can be of use in the meantime to give full scope to the meaning of postcolonial concepts, especially the subaltern, they can expect that a reader will be found to "internalize" or "feel" the concept. I may add, this frequently happens in a fair way of producing reflection and observation, with a variety of scenarios, in every narration. The inferiority of women in relation to their husbands (as was the case with Okonkwo who would oppress and beat up his third wife); the unequal balance of power between father and son (viz., the cruel and suspicious Okonkwo, and the young Nwoye); the difference between masculinity, as an evident sign of strength, and femininity, as an instance of weakness (for that was Okonkwo's attitude toward the behavior of his father Unoka); the punishment of Okonkwo by the lash of the colonial official towards the end of the novel; the sense of the inferiority of the people during the war of the cultures— European and African—which distinguished between the civilized nations and the disorderly, uncivilized people—all these events are strong examples in support of this purpose.

In short, I should affirm that this novel helps to spread postcolonial ideas through the common course of narration, from the union of so many divergent perspectives, which present to them the consequences of empathy, by serving as the first "canals" to convey the power of imagination to their readers. The temptation is stronger to make use of enlarged sentiments, which do honor to human nature, and which ought to enter more deeply into the psyche—that is, in plain terms, the psychology of the emotions buried in the subconscious ocean, so to speak—and to redouble their first-hand knowledge of the present subject in their soul-searching journey, rather than to inculcate decolonial approaches.

Of the Balance of Argument

Were the question proposed, Which of these types of writing, the simple academic piece or the refined novel, is most advantageous to the further decolonization of all past and present offenses, especially after any distinction between the greatness of the colonizers and the unhappiness of the colonized has been abolished? In general, the more the postcolonial questions are inspected in these postmodern times, the less difficulty will a revolutionary meet with in malting and brewing the functions of decolonization, or, what is the same thing, the method of balancing the unequal division of power among the parties concerned. However, as in our previous reasonings, I would beg leave to make a recommendation to truth-seekers—viz., that they have the rarely conjoined merit of those who have approached the subject of postcolonialism with a literary and academic eye in the same manner and who have in the general course of things enjoyed the benefits of these productions. They benefit because academics exercise a rigorous set of rules of analysis, which they intend to convert into actionable policies, beyond the immediate effects of that profession. Frequent instances of a like nature occur in the records of the elucidations of Robbie Shilliam's celebrated opinion on "deep relations," by which the subaltern ought to be raised to the level of the whole "cosmos,"[5] as well as of Gayatri Chakravorty Spivak's later notion, esteemed by Drucilla Cornell,[6] of the obligation to the transformation of colonizers, for the sake of the subaltern. Yet, even if we consider the consequences of these measures, there seem to be obstacles which would be sufficient to prevent the progress of things.

Things Fall Apart, in Achebe's own words,[7] happens to draw the bond of allegiance which unites, "cosmologically" speaking, the interest of the whole collective body of the subaltern in any age or country of the world. In the letters of the Koreans to Achebe, he remembers passages, speaking of the same consequences of colonization—of Imperial Korea by the Empire of Japan in the year 1905—as comprehended, I suppose, by history: a strong proof of how deeply rooted these subaltern relations of colonization are throughout all the cosmos."[8]

Figure 13.2. Antonio Gramsci in 1933.

We come now to the transformation of colonizers that Spivak proposed to consider. In this respect, novels awaken and stimulate general readers, by a miraculous interposition, because they ascertain and expressly point out to the persons engaged in that labor the more intricate and obscure conclusions of postcolonial calculations. For to return to our supposition regarding the augmenting of sympathy and compassion for the "other" members of society, the colonizer must feel an increase of humanity from the very habit of understanding the sense of the subaltern disadvantage; as we may particularly observe in *Things Fall Apart*, which is to a great extent the guide of reason and equity, containing a very exact detail of the most remarkable aspects of pre-colonial life and manners in its native country—a proof that sometimes the stories propagated to the public, cultivated with superior skill in wonderful characterizations, have the depth of the principles upon which humankind, including the subaltern and colonial powers, proceed.

Shilliam and Spivak, though they regard the methods of decolonization last mentioned as extremely useful to the encouragement of emancipation, admit of the influence of the novel here upon the whole connection of decolonial causes and the happy effects without the assistance of academic writings. In my opinion, there is no manner of reason for the complexity of argument—so much illustrated by the subaltern's peripheral "situated knowledge,"[9] which is chiefly maintained by structural "power relations,"[10] and the foundations of "cultural hegemony,"[11] or, if you will, the prevailing ideologies, that they have to overcome—which each party may make use of in order to obtain some account of their conjectural solutions. A very small degree of observation suffices to teach us that science, whether hard or soft, cannot possibly be considered as objective (and detached from life), even though this desire seems the foundation of most of its private passions and interests. It may be thought an instance of vanity that a reader, instead of enriching themselves by the internalization of postcolonial questions through the ordinary course of literary fiction, pretends at all to navigate those received notions in philosophical compositions.

But we know that, in their endeavor to open the door to other discourses or situated knowledges, scholarly works seek to think as well as to act outside the box, if not perhaps to attain the meaningful comprehension of such subjects. Thus, upon comparing the whole, it seems possible that, we could have here evidently the first introduction to other subaltern groups along with the most wretched of the colonized parts of the world, comprehending homosexuals, transsexuals, women, peasants, migrants, etc. Not to mention that the more elaborate novelists, when examined, will be found to make it their chief study to find in these discourses much fertile soil and climate, whence to invent stories more effectually to public advantage. What I have argued here is, therefore, more about the thinking process that goes through the mind when reading, thinking, and writing academic papers.

Idea of a Perfect Balance

To conclude plainly with my inquiry concerning the benefit of academic writings and literature in relating postcolonial questions: as I am a man (I think), both sources enable the public to make the best advantage of novels and scholarly texts in their intercourse with each other. As I am a postmodern traveler, I observe that novels, like *Things Fall Apart*, render postcolonial concepts intelligible to all parties, and such is the force of every art that the generality of humankind would strengthen its resolution to carry into execution their decolonizing intentions. As I am a gay Anglo-Iranian-Romanian, I calmly extol the usefulness of academic folio volumes, since the reading of them necessarily requires so much attention, and forces modern writers and readers to push their subaltern or intellectual boundaries. And notwithstanding that there is a perpetual flux of postcolonial novels to neocolonial countries in the English language, it is not likely we shall find many of the kind that exceed, or even live up to Achebe's oeuvre;[12] whereas, those which are written in all indigenous languages, according to the established mode of the culture of their land, a practice which Ngũgĩ wa Thiong'o has cherished and promoted,[13] may be altogether unknown to all foreign nations. It appears, however, from many autobiographies, such as we observe in Parry's conceptual autoethnography,[14] that the two extremities of literature and academia combine almost every excellence which belongs to the artist's vision and the scholar's methodological rigor.[15] That they have achieved their desired goal remains a topic for another book. I leave to future ages, on any account, to draw their own picture of that luxury which is disposed to suture a proper balance or counterpoise to the principles of success in every conceptual autoethnography; which, in my opinion, is of all postcolonial writings incomparably the best.

ENDNOTES

[1]   Chinua Achebe, "Achebe Discusses Africa 50 Years After 'Things Fall Apart,'" by Jeffrey Brown, *PBS News*, May 27, 2008, https://www.pbs.org/newshour/show/achebe-discusses-africa-50-years-after-things-fall-apart.

[2]   Achebe, "Achebe Discusses Africa 50 Years After 'Things Fall Apart.'"

[3]   Edward W. Said, *Orientalism* (London: Penguin Books, 2003), xiii.

[4]   Sankaran Krishna, "Forgetting Caste While Living It: The Privileges of Amnesia," in *Caste in Life: Experiencing Inequalities*, ed. D. Shyam Babu and R. S. Khare (Delhi, India: Pearson, 2011), 7–19.

[5]   Robbie Shilliam, *The Black Pacific: Anti-Colonial Struggles and Oceanic Connections* (London: Bloomsbury Academic, 2015), 13–33.

[6]   Drucilla Cornell, "The Ethical Affirmation of Human Rights: Gayatri Spivak's Intervention," in *Can the Subaltern Speak? Reflections on the History of an Idea*, ed. Rosalind C. Morris (New York: Columbia University Press, 2010), 110.

[7]   Achebe, "Achebe Discusses Africa 50 Years After 'Things Fall Apart.'"

[8]   Achebe, "Achebe Discusses Africa 50 Years After 'Things Fall Apart.'"

[9]   Donna Haraway, "Situated Knowledges: The Science Question in Feminism and the Privilege of Partial Perspective," *Feminist Studies* 14, no. 3 (Fall 1988): 575–599, https://doi.org/10.2307/3178066.

[10]   Michel Foucault, *Power/Knowledge: Selected Interviews and Other Writings 1972–1977*, ed. Colin Gordon, trans. Colin Gordon and Others (New York: Pantheon Books, 1980).

[11]   Antonio Gramsci, *Selections from the Prison Notebooks*, ed. and trans. Quintin Hoare and Geoffrey Nowell Smith (New York: International Publishers, 1971).

[12]   For instance, Prof. Naeem Inayatullah criticizes *The Kite Runner* by Khaled Hosseini with some vehemence, as it has displayed postcolonial questions in the loosest and most careless manner; Naeem Inayatullah, "Pulling Threads: Intimate Systematicity in *The Politics of Exile*," *Security Dialogue* 44, no. 4 (August 2013): 331–345, https://www.jstor.org/stable/26302240.

[13]   Ngũgĩ wa Thiong'o, *Decolonising the Mind: The Politics of Language in African Literature* (Nairobi, Kenya: East African Educational Publishers, 1986).

[14]   David William Parry, "Cultivating Presence" (PhD diss., University of South Wales, 2025).

[15]   Himadeep Muppidi, *The Colonial Signs of International Relations* (New York: Columbia University Press, 2012), 11–25; Naeem Inayatullah, "Falling

and Flying: An Introduction," In *Autobiographical International Relations: I, IR*, ed. Naeem Inayatullah (Abingdon, UK: Routledge, 2011), 1–12; Inayatullah, "Pulling Threads"; Krishna, "Forgetting Caste While Living It," 7–19.

CHAPTER XIV

Marjane Satrapi's *Persepolis* is an adaptation of her autobiographical graphic novel. Every one knows the event of this animated film: the coming of age of Marjane, an Iranian girl during the whole time of the Islamic Revolution of 1979; going over to Vienna after the revolution; returning to the Islamic Republic of Iran (IRI) thirdly, to Europe afterwards. *Persepolis* is a very comfortable reflection for the more passionate favorers of the Pahlavi monarchy, while her bourgeois views about religion have rendered women tame and abject, and fitted them for subjection. In the meantime she appears to have had the genuine sentiments of middle-class Persians in their affection for the utmost liberty of the market and the distribution of social justice in the eyes of her millennial audiences; for, the graphic novels were published in 2000–2003, and the film in 2007.

Gradually her judgment underwent a change during the course of several years. Yet we may entertain a suspicion that those who defend the established prejudices against the enemies of the despotic power of the United States—which is wholly imperialistic, wholly monstrous and gigantic—would gladly propagate any propagandist story, as in the most shameless stereotypical cinematic representations, such as *Argo* (2012), *Homeland* (2013), *24* (2010), *Syriana* (2005), to the disadvantage of their antagonists. Not to mention, that unnecessary wars—for instance, the Vietnam War (1955–1975) and the Second Gulf War (2003–2011)—scandalous treaties, such as the expansion of the North Atlantic Treaty Organization (NATO) even after the dissolution of the Union of Soviet Socialist Republics (USSR) and the Treaty of Friendship,

Cooperation and Mutual Assistance (TFCMA), or the Warsaw Pact (WP), and every kind of maladministration (beside the assassination of their adversaries, including Fidel Alejandro Castro Ruz of the Republic of Cuba)— may be ascribed to this country. For my part, I will venture, in this seminar, to examine the seeming portrayal of Iran as the subject of controversy, the difference between Iran and Western nations, the observations of feminism in the very nature of the country, the proper signification or symbol of the veil, and some general criticisms against the film.

Figure 14.1. Ruhollah Khomeini's return to Iran in 1979.

Advertisement

I shall first mention that what rendered *Persepolis* chiefly admirable, was that visual and graphic quality, which, at first sight, seems suitable to our age. "The more iconic," says that cartoonist and comics theorist, Scott McCloud, "or abstract an image is the more easily readers are able to identify with it." I believe, therefore, that notwithstanding the great decline of that polite and passionate part of the world, with the noble remains of ancient times, once raised to the love of distant regions, of flying carpets, of desert landscapes, of opulent palaces, of exotic marketplaces, and of harems, which were represented in the paintings of Jean-Léon Gérôme, Jean-Auguste-Dominique Ingres, Nasreddine Dinet, Ferdinand Victor Eugène Delacroix, John Frederick Lewis, Vasily Vereshchagin, Ludwig Deutsch, Rudolf Ernst, Marià Fortuny, and others of the same kind! it is probable, that the bias of the neoconservative elites of the United Kingdom, the United States, and the State of Israel, leans towards the fortunes of the arms industry, the militarization and securitization of ever more private or public affairs, and foreign intervention in the Republic of Iraq, the State of Palestine, the Republic of Lebanon, the Syrian Arab Republic, and Iran, according to the supposition of *A Clean Break: A New Strategy for Securing the Realm*; they are, therefore, most supported by the steady application of political public relations campaigns, like the *September Dossier*, or *Iraq's Weapons of Mass Destruction: The Assessment of the British Government*, in order to administer hegemony in the Middle East and depress the deluded fanatics in this region, even though their fundamentalists are no more enlightened than the Evangelicals in the Bible Belt; but who, what is more strange, have not as yet been able to enter into the common train of Abrahamism, which, indeed, carries the Islamic religion; and it would be folly to regard it as a single denomination, with no other distinguishing branches (Shiism, Sufism, Sunni Islam) as in all others.

Figure 14.2. The interior of the seventh-century mosque of Amr ibn al-As Mosque in Cairo painted by Jean-Léon Gérôme.

East and West

Apart from these additions, the inconsistency between the Western front and her Eastern grounds remains an important theme of the movie, which constantly recurs. In her account of the fact that her punk friends in Vienna ask Marjane if she has seen dead bodies, her interrogators admit in their answer, that her affirmation is "cool." The whole transaction and narrative are emblematic of the specific character that Marjane ascribes to people in Europe, who, for various reasons, are generally not a little superficial in their inclinations in comparison with the many fallen under the ban of the tyrants of the russet plains of Persia, which in self-defense sent its eager sons to war against Ba'athist Iraq—a conflict that lasted from 1980 to 1988: this was one year after the revolution. Marjane's particular friends may be ignorant, by which it is implied they, as well as the majority of people, know not the truth of the world. In everything else the pains of the ancient people of Iran contrast mainly with her contemporaries, whose minds, unmoved and unconcerned, they lull.

Feminism

But the mind of man and woman is also subject to the common sense of feminism during the whole time of the uncensored film (for that was the common course of the limited screenings in Tehran). Indeed, this can be illustrated time and time again by looking at various stages in the movie. During her youth, there are instances where Marjane takes a fancy to become a disciple of Bruce Lee, or an ambitious, or rather a vainglorious, prophetess, when she has grown into an adult: images which bear some resemblance to the manner and character of men of her time. Therefore she cannot but believe that women and men are equal in merit, which would be contrary to the institutions, customs, feelings and beliefs of patriarchy. Simply and constitutionally, as she explains shortly afterwards, she was disappointed when she finds her boyfriend in mischief, who has committed a breach of trust in cheating on her on the day of her birthday. In short, it follows that her broken spirit would not permit her to see the end of all further care about men or their oppressive way. An enemy would have been far less partial! when the vast majority of men are not included in her list.

A few remarks may still be made on the subject of the hijab, and the much-suffering heroines. A general belief prevails that the head covering symbolizes the comparative worthlessness and frailties of women. As Cawley correctly penetrates the meaning of this antithesis, Satrapi both believes that the Western criticism is to be interpreted literally, that there is objection to the liberties of feminism, and that "the usual Western representations of the passive, veiled woman who needs Western intervention to be rescued" are not above suspicion, because daughters of reason were committed to the freedom of expression without the consent of their men. Specific examples might be quoted in support of Cawley's position. Marjane, for instance, exclaims a word of direct remonstrance against the lecturer in Tehran.

To Mrs. Satrapi

Succeeding audiences, as it happened in some countries, such as the Republic of Lebanon, undertook to criticize the film, which they vehemently denounced as "offensive to Iran and Islam," in the zeal they bore for the national interests of their ally. This assertion was not strict truth, and a government should not have prevented all further inquiry; and it must be this passage, if anything, that omits to mention the misery entailed upon the people of Iran by the political doctrine of her native land. When all these things are considered, it would be absurd to assume that Marjane portrayed, in her production, her country's worst qualities. Upon the whole, one may observe that this sort of film, despite the antique coloring, the dramatic forms, and the lively details, is in all times, so far from being the symbolical expression of the fact that the governmental obliquities were produced by the theocratic confluence of clergymen. In the details of her description, let us however confess, that Marjane displays a profound respect for the most authentic history of her identity and the true reflections of her grandmother and her uncle, whose advice, determined her to remember her birth and parentage.

After the conclusion of *Persepolis*, it is but justice to add, that the montage is truly entertaining, considering the locality of the film. Among the emanations of this created text are the details of that canvas' feminism, the orthodoxy of the veil, the impression of the people whose gloomy reign she enumerated, the difference betwixt the West and the Middle East, and a critique of the general theme of the movie. The external evidence leaves no doubt as to its internal authenticity: one unexpected confirmation of the genuineness of the writer's autobiography. Mrs. Satrapi is a contributor to the adequate representation of Iran and the populace of Iran in particular, which is absolutely necessary for others to be acquainted with, for then the world is established in safety.

CHAPTER XV

A RADICALLY FICTIVE ECLOGUE:
IN IMITATION OF DENG XIAOPING'S SPEECH TO THE PARTY
PLENUM OF NOVEMBER 1978, WRITTEN BY IRANDOOST FOR AN
ABERYSTWYTH UNIVERSITY SEMINAR

I trust, Comrades, that notwithstanding the austerity of our late Chairman, your good judgment will incline you to the side of conciliation with the United States. But I confess, it would be wrong to think of the distinctly modern tone of my ideas of openness as those of a thoroughgoing reformer. I think we have travelled only where the revolution gave us light, resolving to deal vigorously not only with Chiang Kai-shek but with his lifelong sympathizers since the Revolution of 1949. If we are proud of our nation, we must not lose forever this time and these chances, which are to arise from this day forward; because after all our struggle for liberty, the first thing that we have to consider with regard to the welfare of the People's Republic of China is a long and arduous course of enterprise, surrounded by an abundance of internal and external enemies who are ready to regulate and restrict the revolution. It is needless to say that the imperialists generally have succeeded in having their own way in some other parts of the East. If we do not succeed, we are without recourse.

It happens, you know, that the rising tide of Communism remains unchanged—but the fact is that we cannot govern through indolence, short-sightedness, and obstinacy. Hitherto, we have seen the hardship of want in People's Republic of China on a large scale. In the Celestial Empire, however, the cadres are as a unit in support of the party, and preparations for the regulation of the stagnating economy should begin in dead earnest. The plan which I shall endeavor to suggest requires that a more effective means than the present reliance on hardy industry should be employed. Ours is a glorious, continuous revolution, which did not end with the Chinese Communist Revolution. To us, the year 1949 marked the beginning of our active struggle between Communism and capitalism; necessary acts done on the hinge of great revolutions for generations to come; and, for my part, I am well sensible that a good deal more is still to be done with regard to our common destiny. Comrades, let me say that I have confidence in the thoroughgoing reforms which I propose.

Figure 15.1. President and Mrs. Ford, Vice Premier Deng Xiao Ping, and Deng's interpreter have a cordial chat during an informal meeting in Beijing, China.

Spring: The First Pastoral, or Economic Situation[1]

My plan, being formed upon the question of regulating the economy, may disappoint (with something more of doubt as to the productive nature of our policy hitherto) some party members. To this objection I answer, that our former methods of securing the state's industrial production are not properly disposed toward our purposes in the great contests for prosperity, at least in the present stage of the affairs of nations, whether they be developed or underdeveloped. Is it not true that there is a very wide difference (why, nearly ten, twenty, or even fifty years' worth, in some areas) in trade and new industries, between China and the cunning fox of the Global North? You will now, Comrades, not think it unnatural that I feel our cause lost, if we cannot adopt our mode of Socialist transformation. Your children will not be supplied, and may falter in their steadfast adherence to our idea of a revolution; whereas, whatever is got by the charter of capitalism, because progressive, will speed in the matters of science, technology, and economy.

Communism depends upon and cannot survive without widespread readjustment and adaptation to carry out its mission of pushing the East Wind, which will go far toward prevailing over the West Wind. Such is the wisdom of our ideas of prudence and accommodation to our present circumstances. The more moderate among the opposers of conciliation are prompted by an incomplete and inaccurate perception of existing institutions. I do confess I looked upon the Gang of Four (Jiang Qing, Mao Zedong's last wife; Zhang Chunqiao; Yao Wenyuan; and Wang Hongwen), and was suspicious of the blunt statement that the policy reforms sought blindly to worship foreign things. I do think, Comrades, that they were wrong in affirming that the conciliation—favored by Zhou Enlai and other members of our party—leaned too much toward the exigencies of capitalist enterprise. In fact, however, our ideas of reform, founded—as far as we are capable of discerning—upon the soundest principles of Socialism, can hardly reject the very foundation of Marxism-Leninism and Maoism (or Mao Zedong Thought). They complain that any one instance of reform is not judicious; I answer that pragmatism is the true remedy for this most ancient nation's disorders.

Comrades, let me, before I choose to enter into the labyrinth of intricate detail, reflect that, for the present, notwithstanding the great strength of our people, nor the determination and resources of our country—the present aspect of our politics has plunged the economy into continual agitation. Here is my first example. Japan is a nation qualified to carry on its annual production of six million tons of steel, to be sure, yet the whole of the force and vigor of its industry is derived from an assembly of six hundred administrators. On the other hand, the Anshan Iron and Steel Group Corporation gave us the same weight of steel, which is nothing less than the labor of twenty-three thousand managerial personnel. We cannot,

Comrades, dread change. Our project is rather designed for promoting the productive forces, and almost immediately respecting the fundamental principle of "each according to his work": indeed, to enable the Communist Party of China to give the working people such assistance as may be a proper incentive and reward for them to exert themselves with more vigor; and be assured the principle at stake—"each according to his work"—will not be carried into the capitalism of the imperialists. (In all, a salary of one or two hundred renminbi is not fit to turn a wheel in the capitalist machine.) The more developed an economy becomes, the more income will it have; the more the worker earns, the more—and the better—will the economic condition flourish.

Summer: The Second Pastoral, or Evidence[2]

Here, Comrades, I plainly perceive by your manner that you object to the effect of this plan, because, you answer, the reform hinders the proper execution of the schemes which you, of yourselves, had proposed. This complaint is nothing but what is natural. I am sensible that it is not easy, indeed, to make advances towards our noble object; for, observe that, besides the desire which all men have of receiving, not without applause, great honors and great medals, for acts that execute the orders of government, especially where a material incentive has been present, it does in a manner frequently happen that the division of labor follows the train of specialism. Our founding father, Karl Marx, was convinced that there are but two ways of dividing labor. In this auspicious scheme specialization does not institute an incurable alienation of capitalism's "repetitive" division of labor. The second mode under consideration is to compel, by the necessity of things, the "social" division of labor, the practice of which is critical to reaching Communism's goals. Truly, this policy will harmoniously dispose the whole mass of the national interest in favor of the working people. Our project is rather designed for making this Celestial Empire the great and flourishing nation that it ought to be. Besides, your living standards can never be advanced an inch before the progressive increase of our economic reproduction is secured.

Comrades, I cannot prevail on myself to hurry over a second consideration. I am particularly compelled to recollect that, the mismanagement committed here has restricted the net produce of our plantations and industries. So far, we have not put in operation the full sweep and breadth of the people's potential. I propose, by decentralizing the economy, and by imposing more responsibilities on the people, to entrust authority to workers; and (far from falling into disorder) to motivate them to think better, and work with a more stubborn spirit. The truth of this observation is seen in such instances as the Great Leap Forward (1958–1962) and the Cultural Revolution (or, if you please, the Great Proletarian Cultural Revolution, 1966–1976), neither of which gave satisfaction to our people concerning the production of goods, in spite of some degree of success. They lacked the professionalism, specialism, and bureaucracy that we are accustomed to find in commercial nations. But, in our present situation, the rural peasants who were likewise armed with new powers were more successful than the rest, as they were aroused and stimulated to the homebred sense of initiative. You will not think it unnatural to protest against compounding any further experiments which tend to the conservation of our national revenue. Let me add that our economy and our management do relate to modes altogether different. Management implies decentralization; and where the economy belongs to state decentralization does in a manner always imply a better method of serving the whole people. Through the public ownership of the means of production, a Socialist system is enforced; and nowhere is there a hint of a bourgeoisie wilderness.

Adhering, as I do, to our policy of relaxing our borders to foreign trade, as well as to the reasons for the Four Modernizations (of agriculture, industry, defense, and science and technology), which had been introduced by Zhou Enlai, our late Premier of the State Council of the People's Republic of China, in 1963, I think that a great deal is still to be done to expedite the exercise of his tract. I only wish you to recognize, in our conjectures of the future, the circumstances—notably, the general development of science and technology—that contribute no mean part towards the growth of national prosperity. We cannot, I fear, invigorate the springs of modern agriculture, industry, and defense without due attention to the fire of science and extent of technology.

Autumn: The Third Pastoral, or Technology and Progress[3]

These, Comrades, are my reasons for opening our doors to the foreign sale of our commodities. I know no other systematic proceeding more completely imprudent than for a political party to insist upon stringent regulations that block up our doors and preclude the wisdom of our deliberative capacity.

Much may be learned about the strength and sharpness of all foreign powers by knowing their modern systems. I look upon the question of conciliation as a sort of historical favor, by which we, who once set about such widespread innovations—including paper, printing, gunpowder, and the compass—are put in possession of technological revolutions. China, once a great nation, innovated many great things; and this share of the proletariat in the universal progress of science and technology must never fail to inspire us with the sentiments and ideas of every opportunity offered.

We are fortunate enough to have begun in earnest the reform of the entry standards at our universities. If we are anything, it is the education, the training, and the evaluation of those students who will answer the leading questions of the consummate knowledge of human progress. In every student exchange program, the student will be allowed to discover new projects and distinctive qualities of mind for the common defense and support of the Chinese communion. In opposing this policy, the Gang of Four believed in the virtue of manual labor, and insisted that scientists were appointed by the bourgeoisie to carry out their capitalist mission of increasing the gross profits they derived from the revenue of the imperial empire. But in truth, this dread of the hostile effect of a group of scientists has no foundation in nature; for science makes no class distinctions. The sense of capitalists is to use these people in favor of capital; whereas our present theme is the mode of Chinese Socialism, which promotes the union of the whole mass of the proletariat, not unmixed with scientists. If the Gang of Four had not stopped us in our course ten years ago, our present desperate situation might have been avoided. The time has come for us to prove that we have a right to render our people prosperous.

Besides, to speak the plain truth, the great object of these measures is to help other Socialist states, since, in the midst of their revolt against imperialism, colonialism, and capitalism in general, we ought to elevate our masses to the greatness of proletarian internationalism. I have therefore set my foot in the tracks of our founding fathers, who dictated the policy of international Socialism, and bequeathed to us the inheritance of so flourishing an undertaking. For, I wish the developed and developing states to be persuaded that Communism, and not capitalism, stands wholly at the end of historical materialism. Accordingly, in the present stage of the dictatorship of the proletariat, the ultimate extension of science and technology is the first definite mover of Marxism-Leninism. When we speak of the longitudinal rate of growth of our productive forces, Socialism cannot lag behind capitalism. Else why all these inextricable difficulties, modifications, and assurances?

The question is, what would be the happy resolution of our Great Helmsman? The chief characteristics of the late Chairman Mao's political philosophy were penetrated with the adaptability and flexibility of a veteran statesman. I would point out for your attention a motto in four words composed by the Great Leader for the Central Party School in Yan'an (Shaanxi): that is, "seek truth from facts." The Chinese Revolution in this respect was led to success through the concrete practice of the universal charter of Marxism-Leninism, and the victorious lesson of the Red Sun's far-sighted vision of systematic pragmatism.

Winter: The Fourth Pastoral, or the Memory of Mao[4]

Lastly, it must be borne in mind that the greater part of the Teacher Mao's thought, having an enlarged view of what is, what is past, and what is to come, was prepared for the support of the public. Indeed, we have been enabled, by understanding the distinctly modern tone of the Four Modernizations— favored by our Great Supreme Commander, and passed by Number Five, Zhou Enlai—wholly to get rid of that most obnoxious representation by the Gang of Four, or others, of the spirit of progress. The problem, at the moment, is that the people's thinking has become rigid, a fact that became more apparent with the ridiculous accusations of the Gang of Four and others. I would state that, as far as it goes, we need a rigid system of "less talk, more action."

Comrade Mao believed in the necessity of revolution, promotion of production, and preparation for war. The Four Modernizations depended upon—and could not be carried out without—adequate reform; and when the burdens imposed in consequence of embargoes were added to the peculiar circumstances of our country, matters went from bad to worse, immediately after the Gang of Four had regarded his instructions as a "national betrayal" and "fawning on foreigners," which marked the beginning of the "capitalist restoration." All these preposterous objections were so interwoven that they did thus seal off the country from the outside world, although it has now ceased to be so completely. I do not dread change and am of the opinion that current international circumstances are appropriate for the occasion in part, or in whole, by the use of foreign capital sources, uniform technology, and profitable experience in business management. It is certainly true that foreign enemies may gain a paltry advantage over us. For instance, when we import complete plants, they shall endeavor to increase the price of their inferior articles; or, if they please, to treat them as better ones. My resolutions, therefore, mean to establish the reforms practically without idolizing any given abstractions and unresolved theoretical principles in debate, like the contemplative Wenchang Wang. Thus, we must act as the chief agents of Erlang Shen, determinedly and attentively, in order to counterbalance the ground of the widening material difference between us and them.

Recommendatory Conclusion[5]

Various things have been suggested as reasons for the reform and the impartial administration of our economy: the march of our technological and productive inventions is slow; I can make no insurance against the voluntary stream of foreign aggression and the subversion of public and private equality without the sanction of the Four Modernizations. There is little doubt that some degree of care and caution is needed in the general handling of such an event, which, with the enemies we are most likely to come to dispute, such as the Gang of Four, will be a matter of delay and much damage to Socialism that cannot be eluded, "like the forwardness of peevish children who, when they cannot get all they would have, are resolved to take nothing." I confess I apprehend that my proposal may not be to your taste, but this is altogether as proper where your criticism seems to signify the great movement of thought. Such keen analysis is characteristic of the people of China, for whose future prosperity and permanent tranquility in all cases whatsoever I have great consideration. If, amidst the moral cause and the bright scene of the glorious revolution, the leadership of the Central Committee of the Communist Party of China raises the banner of Maoism to a higher spirit, I cannot help looking on this event as the strength of our politics, and the unconditional fulfilment of the high calling of our poor peasants and factory workers by the end of the twentieth century.

ENDNOTES

¹   Barry Naughton, "Deng Xiaoping: The Economist," *China Quarterly* 135 (September 1993): 491–514, https://doi.org/10.1017/S0305741000013886; Deng Xiaoping, "The Army Needs to Be Consolidated, January 25, 1975," Selected Works of Deng Xiaoping: Modern Day Contributions to Marxism-Leninism, February 25, 2013, https://dengxiaopingworks.wordpress.com/2013/02/23/the-army-needs-to-be-consolidated/.

²   Deng Xiaoping, "Realize the Four Modernizations and Never Seek Hegemony, May 7, 1978," Selected Works of Deng Xiaoping: Modern Day Contributions to Marxism-Leninism, February 25, 2013, https://dengxiaopingworks.wordpress.com/2013/02/25/realize-the-four-modernizations-and-never-seek-hegemony/; Deng Xiaoping, "Update Enterprises with Advanced Technology and Managerial Expertise, September 18, 1978," Selected Works of Deng Xiaoping: Modern Day Contributions to Marxism-Leninism, February 25, 2013, https://dengxiaopingworks.wordpress.com/2013/02/25/update-enterprises-with-advanced-technology-and-managerial-expertise/.

³   Deng Xiaoping, "Carry Out the Policy of Opening to the Outside World and Learn Advanced Science and Technology from Other Countries, October 10, 1978," Selected Works of Deng Xiaoping: Modern Day Contributions to Marxism-Leninism, February 25, 2013, https://dengxiaopingworks.wordpress.com/2013/02/25/carry-out-the-policy-of-opening-to-the-outside-world-and-learn-advanced-science-and-technology-from-other-countries/; Deng Xiaoping, "Speech at the Opening Ceremony of the National Conference on Science, March 18, 1978," Selected Works of Deng Xiaoping: Modern Day Contributions to Marxism-Leninism, February 25, 2013, https://dengxiaopingworks.wordpress.com/2013/02/25/speech-at-the-opening-ceremony-of-the-national-conference-on-science/.

⁴   Deng, Xiaoping, "Hold High the Banner of Mao Zedong Thought and Adhere to the Principle of Seeking Truth From Facts, September 16, 1978," Selected Works of Deng Xiaoping: Modern Day Contributions to Marxism-Leninism, February 25, 2013, https://dengxiaopingworks.wordpress.com/2013/02/25/hold-high-the-banner-of-mao-zedong-thought-and-adhere-to-the-principle-of-seeking-truth-from-facts/; Deng Xiaoping, "The Working Class Should Make Outstanding Contributions to the Four Modernizations, October 11, 1978," Selected Works of Deng Xiaoping: Modern Day Contributions to Marxism-Leninism, February 25, 2013, https://dengxiaopingworks.wordpress.com/2013/02/25/the-working-class-should-make-outstanding-contributions-to-the-four-modernizations/.

⁵   Deng Xiaoping, "The Whole Party Should Take the Overall Interest into Account and Push the Economy Forward, March 5, 1975," Selected Works of

Deng Xiaoping: Modern Day Contributions to Marxism-Leninism, February 25, 2013, https://dengxiaopingworks.wordpress.com/2013/02/25/the-whole-party-should-take-the-overall-interest-into-account-and-push-the-economy-forward/; Clement A. Tisdell, "Thirty Years of Economic Reform and Openness in China: Retrospect and Prospect" (Economic Theory, Applications and Issues: Working Paper No. 51, University of Queensland, Brisbane, Australia, October 2008), https://doi.org/10.22004/ag.econ.90620.

AN ACKNOWLEDGMENT

The title, *The Dogs of Diplomacy: Exploring the Radical Geography of Modern Times* hardly indicates all that is included in the book, and, I suppose, that I shall offend my readers, if I make some remarks upon it. In short, I had always harbored an aversion for the failings of many schools that seek to reduce to austerity our imagination. If Heaven has so liberally bestowed it on her children, it is not sufficient that they should not turn it to the greatest perfection, as Kant knew so well through the study of philosophy.

After I had spent five years in Wales, I made a second adventure to England, where I completed my second master's in the philosophy of education. It was my intent that my postmodern seminar papers should be published, though I had blotted or lost half of my writings. In the meanwhile, I waited till the ink dried up. And then I relied upon the promises and the heroic care of a family of supporters, whose names I am going to tell you in a short time.

In justification of the greatest learning, I flattered myself with the original writings of travelers, to say nothing of military officers, who passionate and expressive as they were, would take the pains to embrace all the taste of foreign delights through deserts and mountains. Furnished with the tenderness of my dear husband, I took pleasure (if I may say so) in ranging like Colonel T. E. Lawrence (of Arabia) and Captain Richard Francis Burton, from country to country. *All men dream: but not equally. Those who dream by night in the dusty recesses of their minds wake in the day to find that it was vanity: but the dreamers of the day are dangerous men, for they may act their dreams with open eyes, to make it possible.*—At these words I was possessed with so violent an exaltation, that I pressed my husband so earnestly to acquaint me with a thing so very remarkable.

How, he thought, to resolve the matter. How happy should I be if I could write my will across the sky and stars, that his eyes might be shining for me! Lawrence went to S. A. in the Middle East with a desire to learn of men. I came to DWP in England to quiet the disorder of my heart. Burton retired from Victorian morality to sanctify himself in the practice of Sufi virtue. I put myself under the direction of Jesus Christ. With what beauty and elegance of style, though clothed in other languages, they wrote of so many discoveries.

It is fit you should know, that I am no longer deceived by the image of military figures. I am filled, I confess, with the inexorable horror of carcasses, of the treacherous, perfidious murder of other men. That peace pledge which I have signed is a plain declaration of my mind. I recall Jiddu Krishnamurti's words in my memory: "When I kill an Arab, a Jew, a Muslim, a Hindu, a communist, whoever it is, I am killing myself."

But, thanks to Heaven, I think myself hitherto a man who is sensible of his friends, who are infinitely worthy of my acknowledgment. Let me praise their good actions thro' all the world.

I comfort myself by the example of Robert McTeigue, SJ, whose pillared friendship with DWP enlarges my soul, because there appears in him an extraordinary vivacity of zeal and piety, and an aptness for all my philosophical exercises. He will say to me, What are the irregularities of espionage? and what would you say of their salvation? His philosophical toolkits, in *Real Philosophy for Real People: Tools for Truthful Living*, deepens the murmur of the greatest disturbances.[1] So that what Fr. McTeigue says, touches me sensibly.

I thank Stuart Cardell and Mike Riso of Universal Disclosure Podcast (UDP) for the opportunity to converse with them and to acquaint them with my passion![2] They were glad to invite me to their wonderful show upon the promises of the Rev. Parry. They are read and admired, and have resolved to apply themselves wholly to the superior learning of extraterrestrials, and to make marvelous progress in it.

I am earnestly indebted for the trust William Becker (Metaphysical Insights) has for me, owing to the consequence of his sagacious interview. I am grateful, because he took care to give me a liberal occasion for conversation about things somewhat "para" my normal capacities.[3] I received this favor with great joy in the course of Parry's endeavors to bestow on me the first marks of my public exposition.

I cannot help but think of Alan Cox's generosity, who does all things for me and my partner's satisfaction. Heav'n list'n while you converse with

Parry on your weekly broadcasts, as divine service come mended from your tongues.[4]

I thank Paul McFarlane (The Truth Disciples),[5] and Jeff Lippman (Garden Views),[6] for their care, who well understand my discourse; they who incessantly seek for truth in futurities. How void of reason is abundance of persons, you say. You give your disciples reflections in order to free them from those snares which are prepared for the blind.

(I need to try out your forgiveness, my dear reader, lest I should tire you with the repetition of the same motives.)

Gwendolyn Taunton, in my esteem, is the reason that bookshops are often filled with books that refuse to be victims of the least promising plantations. It is easy to censor books and, perhaps, to disrespect the capable intelligence of persons of every age, sex, race, and condition. But I am not ashamed that my regard for my reader's abilities to overcome difficulties and impediments more than any artificial intelligence has had no bounds. Gwendolyn's ship of knowledge, Manticore Press, is the wonder of my age; and being a Shipmistress of the greatest learning, she excels in the ocean of the world, where we can hear of nothing but her sailing sounds, which publish everywhere my letters.

I am thankful to my doctoral supervisors at the University of Glasgow, Comrade Professor Jane Duncan and Professor Bridgette Wessells. I was filled with the inspiration of the university, when they offered to provide the chalice of doctors, so that in a short time I might drink of the cup, even to the bottom. Those who lead a life of more serious studies are scarce. Let them be heard, and do not delay a moment.

I can now do nothing but tell my readers of my utmost love, the most splendid marriage, and the only object of my heart. He (ah! DWP) who loveth with delicacy, from soul to soul! Oh happy state! And raptures of holy joy! Let us sing our songs, like two lovers in the blessed union of their souls! You, whom Nature has qualified for Priesthood in the Church. You are the very reason why I write.

I shall now conclude this radical geography of recent times with a passage from Parry's *Essays* or *Mount Athos Inside Me*:

> Mountains are never, when all said and done, only high-raised geographical peaks. Rather, they are rocky Apostles evoking realities beyond themselves; at the same time as insisting on alpinism both internally and externally. Indeed, they are mineral saints reflecting superconscious worlds,

as well as subtle realms, exceeding the landscape they physically occupy. In this telling fashion, these huge, stony, protagonists equally uplift those who look at them from afar, while demanding reverence from the truly rugged few dwellings thereon. Twin actors, some would say, in a sacred drama promising redemption to frail human flesh. Mutual performers, others might supplement, who participate in the religious rigours necessary to refine multidimensional Consciousness. Still, these granite Landlords refuse to offer the slightest earthly luxury to their hardened tenants. Contrarily, as the marbled ancestors of humankind made adamantine through beatifying pressures, they insist on an honesty of purpose and a vitality of heart.

THE END

ENDNOTES

1   Robert McTeigue, SJ, *Real Philosophy for Real People: Tools for Truthful Living* (San Francisco: Ignatius Press, 2020).

2   David William Parry and Daniele-Hadi Irandoost, "The Secret UAP War: Inside the Intelligence Community," by Mike Riso and Stuart Cardell, *Universal Disclosure Podcast*, January 11, 2025, YouTube video, 1:23:49, https://www.youtube.com/watch?v=w43qs0xV59g.

3   Daniele-Hadi Irandoost, "Metaphysical Insights-Daniele Irandoost- 3-15-25," by William Becker, *William Becker*, March 15, 2025, YouTube video, 57:50, https://www.youtube.com/watch?v=3QeufzwlJB4.

4   Daniele-Hadi Irandoost, "A Spy Special," by Alan Cox, *Alan Cox*, October 25, 2024, YouTube video, 56:35, https://www.youtube.com/watch?v=KmIK40_Zmzs.

5   Daniele-Hadi Irandoost, "Episode 34 – In Conversation with Author Daniele Hadi Irandoost - The Occult Black Art of Espionage and Spying," April 10, 2024, in *The Truth Disciples*, produced by Paul McFarlane, podcast, audio, 1:30:59, https://uk-podcasts.co.uk/podcast/the-truth-disciples/episode-34-in-conversation-with-author-daniele-had.

6   Daniele-Hadi Irandoost, "Garden Views E.88 Spycraft," November 15, 2024, in *Garden Views*, produced by Garden of Doom, podcast, audio, 1:10:08, https://www.spreaker.com/episode/garden-views-e-88-spycraft--62712231.

BIBLIOGRAPHY

Achebe, Chinua. "Achebe Discusses Africa 50 Years After 'Things Fall Apart.' " By Jeffrey Brown. *PBS News Hour*, May 27, 2008. https://www.pbs.org/newshour/show/achebe-discusses-africa-50-years-after-things-fall-apart.

Achebe, Chinua. *Things Fall Apart*. London: Heinemann Educational, 1971.

Archick, Kristin. *The European Parliament*. CRS Report No. RS21998. Washington, DC: Congressional Research Service, 2014. https://sgp.fas.org/crs/row/RS21998.pdf.

Arkoun, Mohammed. "Rethinking Islam Today." *Annals of the American Academy of Political and Social Science* 588, no. 1 (2003): 18–39. https://doi.org/10.1177/0002716203588001003.

Armstrong, David. "The Evolution of International Society." In *The Globalization of World Politics: An Introduction to International Relations*, 5th ed., edited by John Baylis, Steve Smith, and Patricia Owens, 34–49. Oxford: Oxford University Press, 2011.

Armstrong, David. *Revolution and World Order: The Revolutionary State in International Society*. Oxford: Oxford University Press, 1993.

Bălan, Sergiu. "M. Foucault's View on Power Relations." *Cogito—Multidisciplinary Research Journal* 2, no. 2 (2010): 55–61. https://www.ceeol.com/search/article-detail?id=44235.

Barany, Zoltan, and Robert Rauchhaus. "Explaining NATO's Resilience: Is International Relations Theory Useful?" *Contemporary Security Policy* 32, no. 2 (2011): 286–307. https://doi.org/10.1080/13523260.2011.590355.

Barr, Michael. *Who's Afraid of China? The Challenge of Chinese Soft Power*. London: Zed Books, 2011.

BBC News. "British Army in NATO Black Eagle Exercise." November 21, 2014. https://www.bbc.co.uk/news/uk-30142764.

BBC News. "Russian Planes to Patrol in Caribbean, Gulf of Mexico." November 12, 2014. https://www.bbc.co.uk/news/world-europe-30028371.

BBC News. "Viewpoints: European Parliament Powers." July 13, 2010. https://www.bbc.co.uk/news/10598594.

Best, Antony. *Britain, Japan and Pearl Harbor: Avoiding War in East Asia,*

1936–41. London: Routledge, 1995.

Best, Antony, Jussi M. Hanhimäki, Joseph A. Maiolo, and Kirsten E. Schulze. *International History of the Twentieth Century and Beyond*. 2nd ed. Abingdon, UK: Routledge, 2008.

Brabyn, Ben. "Ambition and Humility: Reconnecting Business with Community." Filmed October 2019 in London, UK. TEDx video, 10:18. https://youtu.be/cd1zXVY8EUw?si=Z3qS2L7fsVrXTDHW.

Bull, Hedley. *The Anarchical Society: A Study of Order in World Politics*. New York: Columbia University Press, 1977.

Cammack, Paul. "What the World Bank Means by Poverty Reduction, and Why It Matters." *New Political Economy* 9, no. 2 (June 2004): 189–211. https://doi.org/10.1080/1356346042000218069.

Centre for Air Power Studies. *AP 3000: British Air and Space Power Doctrine*. 4th ed. Norwich: Her Majesty's Stationery Office, 2009.

Child, Ben. "Ben Affleck: Sam Harris and Bill Maher 'Racist' and 'Gross' in Views of Islam." *Guardian*, October 7, 2014. https://www.theguardian.com/film/2014/oct/06/ben-affleck-bill-maher-sam-harris-islam-racist.

Chomsky, Noam. "The Credibility of NATO: Interviewed by Mary Lou Finlay." By Mary Lou Finlay. *As It Happens*, April 16, 1999. https://chomsky.info/19990416/.

Chomsky, Noam. "The Iranian Threat." Chomsky.info. July 2, 2010. https://chomsky.info/20100702/.

Chomsky, Noam. "Militarism, Democracy and People's Right to Information." Lecture given at the Delhi School of Economics, New Delhi, India, November 5, 2001. https://www.india-seminar.com/2002/509/509%20noam%20chomsky.htm.

Cini, Michelle, and Nieves Pérez-Solórzano Borragán, eds. *European Union Politics*. 4th ed. Oxford: Oxford University Press, 2013.

Clark, Ian. "International Society: (ii) Hedley Bull." Lecture given at Aberystwyth University, Aberystwyth, Wales, October 29, 2013.

Cohen, Warren I. "Symposium: Rethinking the Lost Chance in China; Introduction: Was There a 'Lost Chance' in China?" *Diplomatic History* 21, no. 1 (Winter 1997): 71–75. https://www.jstor.org/stable/24913404.

Cornell, Drucilla. "The Ethical Affirmation of Human Rights: Gayatri Spivak's Intervention." In *Can the Subaltern Speak? Reflections on the History of an Idea*, edited by Rosalind C. Morris, 100–116. New York: Columbia University Press, 2010.

Cornell, Svante E. "Religion as a Factor in Caucasian Conflicts." *Civil Wars* 1, no. 3 (Autumn 1998): 46–64. https://www.silkroadstudies.org/resources/pdf/publications/1-religionfactor.pdf.

Deng, Xiaoping. "The Army Needs to Be Consolidated, January 25, 1975." Selected Works of Deng Xiaoping: Modern Day Contributions to Marxism-Leninism. February 25, 2013. https://dengxiaopingworks.wordpress.com/2013/02/23/the-army-needs-to-be-consolidated/.

Deng, Xiaoping. "Carry Out the Policy of Opening to the Outside World and Learn Advanced Science and Technology from Other Countries, October 10, 1978." Selected Works of Deng Xiaoping: Modern Day Contributions to Marxism-Leninism. February 25, 2013. https://dengxiaopingworks.wordpress.com/2013/02/25/carry-out-the-policy-of-opening-to-the-outside-world-and-learn-advanced-science-and-technology-from-other-countries/.

Deng, Xiaoping. "Hold High the Banner of Mao Zedong Thought and Adhere to the Principle of Seeking Truth from Facts, September 16, 1978." Selected Works of Deng Xiaoping: Modern Day Contributions to Marxism-Leninism. February 25, 2013. https://dengxiaopingworks.wordpress.com/2013/02/25/hold-high-the-banner-of-mao-zedong-thought-and-adhere-to-the-principle-of-seeking-truth-from-facts/.

Deng, Xiaoping. "Realize the Four Modernizations and Never Seek Hegemony, May 7, 1978." Selected Works of Deng Xiaoping: Modern Day Contributions to Marxism-Leninism. February 25, 2013. https://dengxiaopingworks.wordpress.com/2013/02/25/realize-the-four-modernizations-and-never-seek-hegemony/.

Deng, Xiaoping. "Speech at the Opening Ceremony of the National Conference on Science, March 18, 1978." Selected Works of Deng Xiaoping: Modern Day Contributions to Marxism-Leninism. February 25, 2013. https://dengxiaopingworks.wordpress.com/2013/02/25/speech-at-the-opening-ceremony-of-the-national-conference-on-science/.

Deng, Xiaoping. "Update Enterprises with Advanced Technology and Managerial Expertise, September 18, 1978." Selected Works of Deng Xiaoping: Modern Day Contributions to Marxism-Leninism. February 25, 2013. https://dengxiaopingworks.wordpress.com/2013/02/25/update-enterprises-with-advanced-technology-and-managerial-expertise/.

Deng, Xiaoping. "The Whole Party Should Take the Overall Interest into Account and Push the Economy Forward, March 5, 1975." Selected Works of Deng Xiaoping: Modern Day Contributions to Marxism-Leninism. February 25, 2013. https://dengxiaopingworks.wordpress.com/2013/02/25/the-whole-party-should-take-the-overall-interest-into-account-and-push-the-economy-forward/.

Deng, Xiaoping. "The Working Class Should Make Outstanding Contributions to the Four Modernizations, October 11, 1978." Selected Works of Deng Xiaoping: Modern Day Contributions to Marxism-Leninism. February 25, 2013. https://dengxiaopingworks.wordpress.com/2013/02/25/the-working-class-should-make-outstanding-contributions-to-the-four-modernizations/.

Diab, Khaled. "The Invasion of Iraq and the Clash Within Civilizations." HuffPost. May 21, 2013. https://www.huffpost.com/entry/clash-of-civilizations-iraq_b_2922448.

Douhet, Giulio. The Command of the Air. Translated by Dino Ferrari. Washington, DC: Office of Air Force History, 1983.

Ehteshami, Anoushiravan. "Islam as a Political Force in International Politics." In Islam in World Politics, edited by Nelly Lahoud and Anthony H. Johns, 29–53. Abingdon, UK: Routledge, 2005.

Engler, Mark. "Defining the Anti-Globalization Movement." Democracy Uprising. April 1, 2007. https://democracyuprising.com/2007/04/01/anti-globalization-movement/.

Fanon, Frantz. *Black Skin, White Masks*. Translated by Charles Lam Markmann. London: Pluto, 1986.

Fanon, Frantz. *The Wretched of the Earth*. Preface by Jean-Paul Sartre. Translated by Constance Farrington. New York: Grove Press, 1963.

Feder, Ellen K. "Power/Knowledge." In *Michel Foucault: Key Concepts*, edited by Dianna Taylor, 55–68. Durham, UK: Acumen, 2011.

Foucault, Michel. *The Archaeology of Knowledge and the Discourse on Language*. Translated by A. M. Sheridan Smith. London: Tavistock Publications, 1972.

Foucault, Michel. *Discipline and Punish: The Birth of the Prison*. 2nd ed., translated by Alan Sheridan. New York: Vintage Books, 1995.

Foucault, Michel. *Politics, Philosophy, Culture: Interviews and Other Writings 1977–1984*. Translated by Alan Sheridan and Others. Edited with an introduction by Lawrence D. Kritzman. New York: Routledge, 1988.

Foucault, Michel. *Power*. Edited by James D. Faubion. Translated by Robert Hurley and Others. New York: The New Press, 2000.

Foucault, Michel. *Power/Knowledge: Selected Interviews and Other Writings 1972–1977*. Edited by Colin Gordon. Translated by Colin Gordon, Leo Marshall, John Mepham, and Kate Soper. New York: Pantheon Books, 1980.

Frank, Andre Gunder. "The Development of Underdevelopment (1969)." In *The Globalization and Development Reader: Perspectives on Development and Global Change*, 2nd ed., edited by J. Timmons Roberts, Amy Bellone Hite, and Nitsan Chorev, 105–114. Chichester, UK: Wiley-Blackwell, 2015.

Gao, Jie. "Compromise and Defence: Great Britain and the Burma Road Crisis." *China and Asia: A Journal in Historical Studies* 3, no. 1 (2021): 5–34. https://doi.org/10.1163/2589465X-030102.

Gareau, Frederick H. "International Institutions and the Gramscian Legacy: Its Modification, Expansion, and Reaffirmation." *Social Science Journal* 33, no. 2 (1996): 223–235. https://doi.org/10.1016/S0362-3319(96)90038-5.

Gawthorpe, Andrew J. " 'Mad Dog?' Samuel Huntington and the Vietnam War." *Journal of Strategic Studies* 41, no. 1–2 (2018): 301–325. https://doi.org/10.1080/01402390.2016.1265510.

Ghannoushi, Soumaya. "Misconceptions of Political Islam." HuffPost. Updated January 16, 2015. https://www.huffpost.com/entry/misconceptions-of-politic_b_6166086.

Grabel, Ilene. "International Private Capital Flows and Developing Countries." In *Rethinking Development Economics*, edited by Ha-Joon Chang, 325–345. London: Anthem Press, 2003.

Gramsci, Antonio. *Selections from the Prison Notebooks*. Edited and translated by Quintin Hoare and Geoffrey Nowell Smith. New York: International Publishers, 1971.

Griffiths, Martin, Terry O'Callaghan, and Steven C. Roach. *International*

Relations: The Key Concepts. 2nd ed. Abingdon, UK: Routledge, 2008.

Gruber, Lloyd. "Globalisation with Growth and Equity: Can We Really Have It All?" *Third World Quarterly* 32, no. 4 (2011): 629–652. https://www.jstor.org/stable/41300339.

Hanson, Victor Davis. "Lord Ismay, NATO, and the Old-New World Order." *National Review*, July 5, 2017. https://www.nationalreview.com/2017/07/nato-russians-out-americans-germans-down-updated-reversed/.

Haraway, Donna. "Situated Knowledges: The Science Question in Feminism and the Privilege of Partial Perspective." *Feminist Studies* 14, no. 3 (Fall 1988): 575–599. https://doi.org/10.2307/3178066.

Hickey, Sam. "Beyond 'Poverty Reduction Through Good Governance': The New Political Economy of Development in Africa." *New Political Economy* 17, no. 5 (2012): 683–690. https://doi.org/10.1080/13563467.2012.732274.

Hix, Simon. "Why the European Parliament Should Not Be Abolished." *European Politics and Policy* (blog), March 5, 2012. https://blogs.lse.ac.uk/europpblog/2012/03/05/why-european-parliament-not-abolished/.

Hix, Simon. "Why the 2014 European Elections Matter: Ten Key Votes in the 2009–2013 European Parliament." *European Policy Analysis* 15 (September 2013): 1–16. https://sieps.se/media/cmfjfa2b/why-the-2014-european-elections-matter_-ten-key-votes-in-the-2009-2013-european-parliament-2013_15epa.pdf.

Hobbes, Thomas. *Leviathan*. Rev. student ed., edited by Richard Tuck. Cambridge: Cambridge University Press, 1996.

Hudson, Valerie M., and Christopher S. Vore. "Foreign Policy Analysis Yesterday, Today, and Tomorrow." *Mershon International Studies Review* 39, no. 2 (October 1995): 209–238. https://doi.org/10.2307/222751.

Huntington, Samuel P. "The Clash of Civilizations?" *Foreign Affairs* 72, no. 3 (Summer 1993): 22–49. https://doi.org/10.2307/20045621.

Inayatullah, Naeem. "Falling and Flying: An Introduction." In *Autobiographical International Relations: I, IR*, edited by Naeem Inayatullah, 1–12. Abingdon, UK: Routledge, 2011.

Inayatullah, Naeem. "Pulling Threads: Intimate Systematicity in *The Politics of Exile*." *Security Dialogue* 44, no. 4 (August 2013): 331–345. https://www.jstor.org/stable/26302240.

Irandoost, Daniele-Hadi. "Episode 34 – In Conversation with Author Daniele Hadi Irandoost - The Occult Black Art of Espionage and Spying." Produced by Paul McFarlane. *The Truth Disciples*, April 10, 2024. Podcast, audio, 1:30:59. https://uk-podcasts.co.uk/podcast/the-truth-disciples/episode-34-in-conversation-with-author-daniele-had.

Irandoost, Daniele-Hadi. "Garden Views E.88 Spycraft." Produced by Garden of Doom. *Garden Views*, November 15, 2024. Podcast, audio, 1:10:08. https://www.spreaker.com/episode/garden-views-e-88-spycraft--62712231.

Irandoost, Daniele-Hadi. "Metaphysical Insights-Daniele Irandoost- 3-15-25." By William Becker. *William Becker*, March 15, 2025. YouTube video, 57:50.

https://www.youtube.com/watch?v=3QeufzwlJB4.

Irandoost, Daniele-Hadi. "A Spy Special." Produced by Alan Cox. *Alan Cox*, October 25, 2024. YouTube video, 56:35. https://www.youtube.com/watch?v=KmIK40_Zmzs.

Iriye, Akira. *The Origins of the Second World War in Asia and the Pacific*. Harlow, UK: Longman, 1987.

Jian, Chen. "The Myth of America's 'Lost Chance' in China: A Chinese Perspective in Light of New Evidence." *Diplomatic History* 21, no. 1 (Winter 1997): 77–86. https://www.jstor.org/stable/24913405.

Kacowicz, Arie M. "Globalization, Poverty, and the North-South Divide." *International Studies Review* 9, no. 4 (2007): 565–580. https://doi.org/10.1111/j.1468-2486.2007.00723.x.

Keylor, William R. *The Twentieth-Century World: An International History*. 4th ed. Oxford: Oxford University Press, 2001.

Kiely, Ray. *Globalization and Postcolonialism: Hegemony and Resistance in the Twenty-First Century*. Lanham, MD: Rowman and Littlefield, 2009.

Kiely, Ray. "Globalization and Poverty, and the Poverty of Globalization Theory." *Current Sociology* 53, no. 6 (2005): 895–914. https://doi.org/10.1177/0011392105057154.

Krishna, Sankaran. "Forgetting Caste While Living It: The Privileges of Amnesia." In *Caste in Life: Experiencing Inequalities*, edited by D. Shyam Babu and R. S. Khare, 7–19. Delhi, India: Pearson, 2011.

Le Carré, John. *A Delicate Truth*. London: Penguin Books, 2014.

Lee, Harper. *To Kill a Mockingbird*. London: Heinemann Educational, 1966.

Lenaerts, Koen "The Principle of Democracy in the Case Law of the European Court of Justice." *International and Comparative Law Quarterly* 62, no. 2 (2013): 271–315. https://doi.org/10.1017/S0020589313000080.

Lessa, Iara. "Discursive Struggles Within Social Welfare: Restaging Teen Motherhood." *British Journal of Social Work* 36, no. 2 (2006): 283–298. https://www.jstor.org/stable/23720912.

Leys, Colin. *Underdevelopment in Kenya: The Political Economy of Neo-Colonialism 1964–1971*. Nairobi, Kenya: East African Education Publishers, 1975.

Linklater, Andrew. "The English School Conception of International Society: Reflections on Western and Non-Western Perspectives." *Ritsumeikan Annual Review of International Studies* 9 (2010): 1–13.

Lynch, Richard A. "Foucault's Theory of Power." In *Michel Foucault: Key Concepts*, edited by Dianna Taylor, 13–26. Durham, UK: Acumen, 2011.

Mao, Tse-tung. "Farewell, Leighton Stuart!" In *The Third Revolutionary Civil War Period*. Vol. 4 of *Selected Works of Mao Tse-tung*, 433–440. Peking: Foreign Languages Press, 1961. https://www.marxists.org/reference/archive/mao/selected-works/volume-4/mswv4_67.htm.

Martins, Nuno. "Globalisation, Inequality and the Economic

Crisis." *New Political Economy* 16, no. 1 (2011): 1–18. https://doi. org/10.1080/13563461003789761.

Marx, Karl. *The Process of Production of Capital*. Vol. 1 of *Capital: A Critique of Political Economy*, translated from the 3rd German ed. by Samuel Moore and Edward Aveling, and edited by Friedrich Engels. Revised and amplified according to the 4th German ed. by Ernest Untermann. Moscow: Progress Publishers, n.d.

Marx, Karl, and Friedrich Engels. "Manifesto of the Communist Party (1948) and Alienated Labour (1844)." In *The Globalization and Development Reader: Perspectives on Development and Global Change*, 2nd ed., edited by J. Timmons Roberts, Amy Bellone Hite, and Nitsan Chorev, 29–38. Chichester, UK: Wiley-Blackwell, 2015.

Masters, Jonathan. "The North Atlantic Treaty Organization (NATO)." Council on Foreign Relations, August 5, 2014. https:// web.archive.org/web/20141223105816/http://www.cfr.org/nato/ north-atlantic-treaty-organization-nato/p28287.

McCalla, Robert B. "NATO's Persistence After the Cold War." *International Organization* 50, no. 3 (Summer 1996): 445–475. https://www.jstor.org/ stable/2704032.

McInnes, Colin. "Fatal Attraction? Air Power and the West." *Contemporary Security Policy* 22, no. 3 (2001): 28–51. https://doi.org/10.1080/13523260512331 3911218.

McInnes, Colin. *Spectator-Sport War: The West and Contemporary Conflict*. Boulder, CO: Lynne Rienner Publishers, 2002.

McTeigue, Robert, SJ. *Real Philosophy for Real People: Tools for Truthful Living*. San Francisco: Ignatius Press, 2020.

Monshipouri, Mahmood, and Manochehr Dorraj. "Iran's Foreign Policy: A Shifting Strategic Landscape." *Middle East Policy* 20, no. 4 (Winter 2013): 133–147. https://doi.org/10.1111/mepo.12052.

Moran, Daniel. "Geography and Strategy." In *Strategy in the Contemporary World: An Introduction to Strategic Studies*, 3rd ed., edited by John Baylis, James J. Wirtz, and Colin S. Gray, 124–140. Oxford: Oxford University Press, 2010.

Mousavian, Seyed Hossein. "Five Options for Iran's New President." *Cairo Review of Global Affairs*, no. 10 (Summer 2013): 68–79. https://crescent.icit-digital.org/ articles/nuclear-energy-for-all-and-nuclear-weapons-for-none-the-rahbar.

Mueller, Julie L. "The IMF, Neoliberalism and Hegemony." *Global Society* 25, no. 3 (2011): 377–402. https://doi.org/10.1080/13600826.2011.577032.

Muppidi, Himadeep. *The Colonial Signs of International Relations*. New York: Columbia University Press, 2012.

Naughton, Barry. "Deng Xiaoping: The Economist." *China Quarterly* 135 (1993): 491–514. https://doi.org/10.1017/S0305741000013886.

Ngũgĩ wa Thiong'o. *Decolonising the Mind: The Politics of Language in African Literature*. Nairobi, Kenya: East African Educational Publishers, 1986.

O'Farrell, Clare. *Michel Foucault*. London: Sage Publications, 2005.

Overy, Richard. "Air Warfare." In *The Oxford History of Modern War*, edited by Charles Townshend, 262–279. Oxford, Oxford University Press, 2005.

Parry, David William. *Caliban's Redemption*. Oxford: Mandrake, 2021.

Parry, David William. "Cultivating Presence." PhD diss., University of South Wales, 2025.

Parry, David William. "Gemini City." In *Voices of Friends Poetry and Art Almanac 2024*, edited by John Farndon, Marina Podlesnaya, and David William Parry. [Hemel Hempstead, UK?]: Hertfordshire Press, 2023.

Parry, David William. *The Grammar of Witchcraft*. Hemel Hempstead, UK: Hertfordshire Press, 2016.

Parry, David William. *Mount Athos Inside Me: Essays on Religion, Swedenborg and Arts*. Melbourne: Manticore Press, 2019.

Parry, David William. *Women in Mayhem: Or Three Nonsensical Pranks*. Melbourne: Manticore Press, 2024.

Parry, David William, and Daniele-Hadi Irandoost. "The Secret UAP War: Inside the Intelligence Community." By Mike Riso and Stuart Cardell. *Universal Disclosure Podcast*, January 11, 2025. YouTube video, 1:23:49. https://www.youtube.com/watch?v=w43qs0xV59g.

Pouliot, Vincent. "The Alive and Well Transatlantic Security Community: A Theoretical Reply to Michael Cox." *European Journal of International Relations* 12, no. 1 (2006): 119–127. https://doi.org/10.1177/1354066106061332.

Prescott, Francis C., Ralph R. Goodwin, Herbert A. Fine, and Velma Hastings Cassidy, eds. *The Far East: China*. Vol. 8 of *Foreign Relations of the United States, 1949*. Washington, DC: United States Government Printing Office, 2010. https://history.state.gov/historicaldocuments/frus1949v08.

Prescott, Francis C., Herbert A. Fine, and Velma Hastings Cassidy, eds. *The Far East: China*. Vol. 9 of *Foreign Relations of the United States, 1949*. Washington, DC: United States Government Printing Office, 1974). https://history.state.gov/historicaldocuments/frus1949v09/d884.

Rajaee, Farhang. *Islamic Values and World View: Khomeyni on Man, the State and International Politics*. Vol. 13 of *American Values Projected Abroad*, with a preface by Kenneth W. Thompson. Lanham, MD: University Press of America, 1983.

Ramo, Joshua Cooper. "The Three Marketeers." *Time*, February 15, 1999. https://time.com/archive/6955233/the-three-marketeers-2/.

Rostow, W. W. *The Stages of Economic Growth: A Non-Communist Manifesto*. 3rd ed. Cambridge: Cambridge University Press, 1990.

Said, Edward W. *Culture and Imperialism*. New York: Vintage Books, 1994.

Said, Edward W. *Orientalism*. London: Penguin Books, 2003.

Scott, Sir Walter. *Rob Roy, Complete, Illustrated*. Boston, 1893; Project Gutenberg, 2018. https://www.gutenberg.org/files/7025/7025-h/7025-h.htm.

Shaffer, Brenda. "The Islamic Republic of Iran: Is It Really?" In *The Limits of Culture: Islam and Foreign Policy*, edited by Brenda Shaffer, 219–239. Cambridge, MA: MIT Press, 2006.

Sheng, Michael M. "America's Lost Chance in China? A Reappraisal of Chinese Communist Policy Toward the United States before 1945." *Australian Journal of Chinese Affairs* 29 (January 1993): 135–157. https://doi.org/10.2307/2949955.

Sheng, Michael M. "Chinese Communist Policy Toward the United States and the Myth of the 'Lost Chance' 1948–1950." *Modern Asian Studies* 28, no. 3 (July 1994): 475–502. https://doi.org/10.1017/S0026749X00011835.

Shilliam, Robbie. *The Black Pacific: Anticolonial Struggles and Oceanic Connections*. London: Bloomsbury Academic, 2015.

Singer, J. David. "The Level-of-Analysis Problem in International Relations." *World Politics* 14, no. 1 (October 1961): 77–92. https://doi.org/10.2307/2009557.

Smith, Adam. *An Inquiry into the Nature and Causes of the Wealth of Nations*. With an introduction by Mark G. Spencer. Ware, UK: Wordsworth Editions, 2012.

Statista. "Voter Turnout in the European Parliament Elections in the European Union (EU) from 1979 to 2024." Released July 2024. https://www.statista.com/statistics/300427/eu-parlament-turnout-for-the-european-elections/.

Stephan, John. Review of *Demystifying Pearl Harbor: A New Perspective from Japan*, by Iguchi Takeo, with a foreword by Akira Iriye. *Journal of Pacific History* 46, no. 1 (2011): 143–144. https://doi.org/10.1080/00223344.2011.573650.

Stokes, Philip. *Philosophy: 100 Essential Thinkers: The Ideas That Have Shaped Our World*. London: Arcturus Publishing, 2012.

Taylor, Dianna, ed. *Michel Foucault: Key Concepts*. Durham, UK: Acumen, 2011.

The Economist. "NATO Flexes Its Muscle Memory." August 30, 2014. https://www.economist.com/international/2014/08/30/nato-flexes-its-muscle-memory.

Tisdell, Clement A. "Thirty Years of Economic Reform and Openness in China: Retrospect and Prospect." Economic Theory, Applications and Issues: Working Paper No. 51, University of Queensland, Brisbane, Australia, October 2008. https://doi.org/10.22004/ag.econ.90620.

Tuchman, Barbara W. "If Mao Had Come to Washington: An Essay in Alternatives." *Foreign Affairs* 51, no. 1 (October 1972). https://www.foreignaffairs.com/articles/china/if-mao-had-come-washington-nixon-tuchman.

Vonnegut, Kurt, Jr. *Slaughterhouse-Five or the Children's Crusade: A Duty-Dance with Death*. London: Vintage, 1991.

Wade, Robert Hunter. "On the Causes of Increasing World Poverty and Inequality, or Why the Matthew Effect Prevails." *New Political Economy* 9, no. 2 (2004): 163–188. https://doi.org/10.1080/1356346042000218050.

Walt, Stephen M. "Why Alliances Endure or Collapse." *Survival* 39, no. 1 (1997): 156–179. https://doi.org/10.1080/00396339708442901.

Waltz, Kenneth N. "Structural Realism After the Cold War." *International Security* 25, no. 1 (Summer 2000): 5–41. https://www.jstor.org/stable/2626772.

Warner, Carolyn M., and Stephen G. Walker. "Thinking About the Role of Religion in Foreign Policy: A Framework for Analysis." *Foreign Policy Analysis* 7, no. 1 (January 2011): 113–135. https://doi.org/10.1111/j.1743-8594.2010.00125.x.

Wearden, Graeme. "Oxfam: 85 Richest People as Wealthy as Poorest Half of the World." *Guardian*, January 20, 2014. https://www.theguardian.com/business/2014/jan/20/oxfam-85-richest-people-half-of-the-world.

Webber, Mark, James Sperling, and Martin A. Smith. *NATO's Post-Cold War Trajectory: Decline or Regeneration?* Basingstoke, UK: Palgrave Macmillan, 2012.

Wedel, Janine R. *Shadow Elite: How the World's New Power Brokers Undermine Democracy, Government, and the Free Market.* New York: Basic Books, 2009.

Wells, H. G. *The War in the Air.* London, 1908; Project Gutenberg, 2024. https://www.gutenberg.org/files/780/780-h/780-h.htm.

Westad, Odd Arne. "Losses, Chances, and Myths: The United States and the Creation of the Sino-Soviet Alliance, 1945–1950." *Diplomatic History* 21, no. 1 (Winter 1997): 105–115. https://www.jstor.org/stable/24913408.

Westad, Odd Arne. "Rivals and Allies: Stalin, Mao, and the Chinese Civil War, January 1949." *Cold War International History Project Bulletin*, no. 6–7 (Winter 1995/1996): 7, 27. https://www.wilsoncenter.org/sites/default/files/media/documents/publication/CWIHP_Bulletin_6-7.pdf.

Westad, Odd Arne. "Unwrapping the Stalin-Mao Talks: Setting the Record Straight." In *Cold War International History Project Bulletin*, no. 6–7 (Winter 1995/1996): 23–24. https://www.wilsoncenter.org/sites/default/files/media/documents/publication/CWIHP_Bulletin_6-7.pdf.

Whisnant, Clayton. "Foucault & Discourse: A Handout for HIS 389." Last modified November 9, 2012. https://web.archive.org/web/20120208013606/http://webs.wofford.edu/whisnantcj/his389/foucault_discourse.pdf.

Whitfield, Lindsay. "How Countries Become Rich and Reduce Poverty: A Review of Heterodox Explanations of Economic Development." *Development Policy Review* 30, no. 3 (May 2012): 239–260. https://doi.org/10.1111/j.1467-7679.2012.00575.x.

Wintour, Patrick. "European Parliament Should Be Abolished, Says Jack Straw." *Guardian*, February 21, 2012. https://www.theguardian.com/world/2012/feb/21/european-parliament-abolish-jack-straw.

Woodward, David. "Democratizing Global Governance for Sustainable Human Development." *Development* 53, no. 1 (2010): 42–47. https://doi.org/10.1057/dev.2009.85.

World Bank. "Poverty Overview." Last updated October 7, 2014. https://web.archive.org/web/20150214050250/https://www.worldbank.org/en/topic/poverty/overview.

Young, Robert J. C. *Postcolonialism: A Very Short Introduction.* Oxford: Oxford University Press, 2003.

Zarif, Mohammad Javad. "What Iran Really Wants: Iranian Foreign Policy in the Rouhani Era." *Foreign Affairs*, April 17, 2014. https://www.foreignaffairs.

com/articles/iran/2014-04-17/what-iran-really-wants.

Zehfuss, Maja. "Conclusion: What Can We Do to Change the World?" In *Global Politics: A New Introduction*, edited by Jenny Edkins and Maja Zehfuss, 610–628. Abingdon, UK: Routledge, 2014.

www.ingramcontent.com/pod-product-compliance
Lightning Source LLC
Chambersburg PA
CBHW031509270326
41930CB00006B/331